Power, Service, Humility

Power, Service, Humility

A New Testament Ethic

Reinhard Feldmeier
Brian McNeil, translator

BAYLOR UNIVERSITY PRESS

Cover Design and Illustration by Hannah Feldmeier

Translator's Note: Biblical passages are quoted from the New Revised Standard Version (Oxford University Press, 1989). Sometimes a more literal translation is given to bring out the author's meaning.

This work was originally published in German as *Macht—Dienst—Demut: Ein neutestamentlicher Beitrag zur Ethik* by Mohr Siebeck (Tübingen, 2012).

Library of Congress Cataloging-in-Publication Data

Feldmeier, Reinhard.
[Macht—Dienst—Demut. English]
Power, service, humility : a New Testament ethic / Reinhard Feldmeier ; Brian McNeil, translator.
155 pages cm
Includes bibliographical references and index.
ISBN 978-1-4813-0025-4 (pbk. : alk. paper)
1. Bible. New Testament—Criticism, interpretation, etc.
2. Power (Christian theology)—Biblical teaching.
3. Devil—Biblical teaching. I. Title.
BS2545.P66F4513 2014
241—dc23

2013020061

Printed in the United States of America on acid-free paper with a minimum of 30% post-consumer waste recycled content.

For
Hannah
Kaspar
Myrta

Contents

Acknowledgments

Acknowledgments are due

to my collaborators who have discussed with me the theses presented in this little book and who have read through its final version: private lecturer Dr. Alexa Wilke, Mr. Felix Albrecht, Ms. Heidrun Gunkel, Mr. Manuel Kaden, and Ms. Inga Mrozek;

to the Lichtenberg Kolleg of the Georg-August-University, which has not only given me the opportunity to have discussions with interesting colleagues but has also made it possible for me to complete this book in good time, thanks to a partial leave of absence from teaching obligations;

to the publishers, Mohr Siebeck and Baylor University Press, and in particular to Dr. Henning Ziebritzki and Dr. Carey Newman, for collaboration that is, as ever, excellent;

to the Benedictine monks of the monastery of Kremsmünster, for their hospitality while the final draft of this book was written;

and finally, to our children, Hannah, Kaspar, and Myrta, for their love in the last three decades. This book is dedicated to them.

Göttingen, June 11, 2012

Reinhard Feldmeier

Prelude with the Devil

"You will be like God"—with this enticement, the serpent comes to the human being after the creation (Gen 3:5) and seduces him into falling away from God. The consequences are drastically illustrated already in the following chapter, when Cain kills his brother Abel. The "prehistory" at the beginning of the Bible makes it clear that the urge to push oneself up too high is so elemental to the human being that the tempter can successfully take hold of him by means of it, and bring about his downfall.[1] This is why Bernard of Clairvaux, the great preacher of humility, advises his pupil Pope Eugene, "No poison or sword ought to terrify you as much as the lust for domination."[2]

It is thus no cause for surprise when the devil applies precisely this lever—the *libido dominandi*, the "will for power"—against Jesus at the beginning of the Gospel story, before he first appears on the public scene.[3] After Jesus has been revealed by God in the baptism as his "beloved Son" and he has prepared himself for the path that lies ahead by fasting for forty days in the desert, the tempter comes to him to interpret in his own way what "the Son of God" means. Like Adam and Eve at the beginning of prehistory, Jesus too must decide at the start of his public ministry what will orient him on his future path.

The temptation consists of three exchanges that are related to each other in the form of a climax. In the first two exchanges, the devil takes up the words addressed by God to Jesus (Matt 4:3, 6).[4] He starts with the most obvious issue: since Jesus is hungry after his lengthy fast, the devil suggests, "If you are the Son of God, command these stones to become loaves of bread." The subtext runs, "What is the point of divinity, other than to satisfy one's own needs?" Jesus counters with a quotation from the Bible: "The human being does not live by bread alone, but by every word that comes from the mouth of God" (Matt 4:4 = Deut 8:3).

But the devil does not give up. In the second exchange, he takes Jesus to the pinnacle of the temple and begins once more with the conditional phrase "if you are the Son of God . . ." This time, his interpretation of the title "Son of God" is more subtle: by jumping from the pinnacle of the temple, Jesus is to demonstrate to all the world that he truly has God on his side. And if Jesus argues by means of quotations from the Bible, then the devil can do the same. In justification, he quotes Psalm 91:11-12: "'He will command his angels concerning you to guard you in all your ways. On their hands they will bear you up, so that you will not dash your foot against a stone.'" Once again, Jesus repulses him with a quotation from the Bible: "You shall not put the Lord your God to the test" (Matt 4:7 = Deut 6:16).

The devil now forgoes further arguments and drops his mask. He leads Jesus to a high mountain, where he offers him the lordship over all the kingdoms of the world—an immediate and comprehensive satisfaction of Adam's craving for power. His only condition is that Jesus shall fall down before him and adore him. In other words, Jesus must submit to him rather than to God.

The devil wants Jesus' divine sonship to be understood as a synonym for superior power. He wants a son without a father, a Son of God without God. For the devil, power per se is divine, power in the sense of an unfettered personal authority. Power of that kind is present everywhere in the world, and this is why, in the Lukan variant of the temptation narrative, the devil can justify his offer to Jesus of lordship over the world by saying that all the kingdoms he is offering him have been "given over" to him (Luke 4:6). The bloody tracks of this kind of power run through the whole of the New Testament canon, from the first book, with Herod's power-driven murder of children in the Gospel of Matthew's infancy narrative (2:16-18), to the description of Rome as the harlot Babylon, drunk with the blood of the saints, in the last book, the Revelation of John (17:1-6; cf. 18:21-24).

Jesus counters the final temptation too with a quotation from the Bible, when he says that the human being should serve God alone and fall down before him (Matt 4:10 = Deut 6:13 LXX). This is his third quotation from the context of the foundational Jewish confession, the *Shema Yisrael.* The core of this confession is the unconditional love for God: "you shall love the Lord your God with all your heart, and with all your soul, and with all your might" (Deut 6:5). Jesus thus makes it clear that, in his eyes, divine sonship consists not in the domination of others but in the fellowship with the Father whom alone he "serves." Since this "service of God" includes the service of human beings, Jesus, toward the end of his life, can sum up his mission as "serving" (Mark 10:45 par. Matt 20:28; Luke 22:27).[5]

When we are told, after Jesus passes the test of the third temptation, that the devil leaves Jesus and the angels come to him and serve him (Matt 4:11), this indicates that from this human being, who makes himself totally subordinate to God, there shines out something of the paradise that the first human being lost. Accordingly, Jesus now makes his public appearance and proclaims that the prophetic promises of salvation have been fulfilled:

> The people who sat in darkness have seen a great light,
> and for those who sat in the region and shadow of death
> light has dawned. (Matt 4:16 = Isa 9:1)

This is what the first Gospel says in one passage that reflects on the story it tells.[6] The prophet's prediction is in the future tense. When it is put in the past, with an aorist verbal form, this presents the prophecy as fulfilled—fulfilled through the one who is no longer (like the prophet) called the "servant of God" but the Son of God.

The rejection of the devil's offers by the Son of God must not, however, be misunderstood as a fundamental renunciation of power. On the contrary, by renouncing any authority of his own, Jesus "possesses in the greatness of God that which bears him and lifts him up. By keeping himself subordinate to God—that is to say, through his humility—he acquires union with him."[7] Jesus' authority is generated by this union with God, and this is why "humility and the consciousness of power constantly compenetrate each other" in Jesus.[8] It is in this way that the conqueror of the tempter can now come on stage in the Gospels and proclaim the irruption of the rule of God.[9] Nor is it only a question of proclamation: when Jesus appears on the scene, God's powerful presence is already breaking into this world and manifesting itself palpably in his authoritative deeds (Matt 4:14; 7:29). Such deeds are demonstrations of power. In particular, the exorcisms show that, through the appearance of Jesus, "the strong man" (i.e., Satan) is "bound" (Matt 12:28-29 par. Mark 3:27). Accordingly, the Gospel bears witness not to a renunciation of power but to a changeover of power. This was announced in the Old Testament,[10] and the testimony of the New Testament proclaims that this takes place through the appearing of Jesus on the scene. This is why in Acts Peter can look back over the entire activity of Jesus and present it as a victory over the power of the devil, made possible by Jesus' fellowship with God:

> That message spread throughout Judea,
> beginning in Galilee after the baptism that John announced:
> how God anointed Jesus of Nazareth
> with the Holy Spirit and with power;
> how he went about doing good and healing
> all who were oppressed by the devil,
> for God was with him. (Acts 10:37-38)

Jesus thus certainly possesses power, but—as this passage explicitly states—the power in which he acts comes as an authority bestowed by his union with God: "God anointed [him] with the Holy Spirit and with power . . . for God was with him." In the Gospel, this power is usually called *exousia* (cf. Matt 7:29; 9:6, 8). Unlike other terms for power, such as *kratos*, *iskhus*, *dunamis*, or *energeia*, which denote the power that dwells in a person and is therefore available to him of its own accord, the noun *exousia*, which is employed for the authority of Jesus, is derived from the impersonal verb *exestin*, "it is possible," "it is allowed," and denotes a right that is granted by someone else, as well as the ability to act that is opened up by this right.[11] Since this *exousia* is bestowed by God, it will never be used by Jesus on his own initiative without any reference to the will of this God (see Matt 9:8).

But Jesus seems to have won only a Pyrrhic victory when he passes the test of temptation. In the end, the devil seems all the more impressively to win the triumph that he failed to get in his dialogue with Jesus: after brief public activity, Jesus is taken captive and—ironically—is crucified as "king of the Jews," that is to say, as a usurper and insurrectionist. The path of the human being Jesus of Nazareth is radically thwarted in the encounter with the power of the civil authorities. The evangelist once again weaves the voice of the tempter into this event, when the crucified Jesus is confronted one last time with his claim to be the Son of God. Initially, it is the passers-by who mock him and challenge him: "Save yourself! If you are the Son of God, come down from the cross" (Matt 27:40). This is repeated somewhat more subtly a second time, when the chief priests, the scribes, and the elders pronounce their verdict on Jesus (now already in the third person, which means that they are addressing the others):

> He saved others; he cannot save himself.
> He is the King of Israel; let him come down from the cross now,
> and we will believe in him.
> *He trusts in God; let God deliver him now, if he delights in him*;
> for he said, "I am God's Son." (Matt 27:42-43)

Like the devil in the second temptation, his henchmen here employ a quotation from Scripture (Ps 22:9). In the Psalm that they quote, his enemies mock the one who prays because of the wretched things that happen to him, so that his only recourse is to lament and ask his God why he has abandoned him (Ps 22:2). In the context of the Gospel, this becomes the apparent refutation of the divine sonship of Jesus. A comparison with Mark 15:29-32, on which Matthew's text is based, shows that the evangelist himself has inserted the double reference to the divine sonship here—first in a literal allusion to the temptation narrative, and then a second time with a scriptural quotation—in order to establish a direct relationship between the crucifixion and the beginning of Jesus' public activity and to interpret it in this way as the "last temptation of Christ."

But the Son of God does not yield to this temptation. The evangelist explicitly tells us, when Jesus is arrested, that he could ask his Father for twelve legions of angels to save him (Matt 26:53), but he does not save himself. Instead, he dies on the cross. This is the end of the life of Jesus, but it is not the end of his story. The obedient path taken by the Son to death on the cross becomes the beginning of the Gospel of Jesus Christ. Matthew hints at this already when Jesus dies and, immediately after his death, the veil of the temple is torn asunder, the rocks are split, the tombs are opened, and the dead appear in the city (Matt 27:51-53). This anticipation of the resurrection at the end of time emphasizes that it is not death and the devil who have the last word in the dying of Jesus, but the God who is the Father to whom Jesus has obediently submitted[12] and who therefore gives Jesus his unconditional support. The mocking echo of the tempter's voice at the crucifixion is thus not the last reference back to the scene of the temptation. Jesus standing once more on a mountain at the close of the Gospel is surely an allusion to the last of the three temptations. Here, too, it is a question of world dominion, as the introduction to his parting words makes clear: "All authority [*exousia*] in heaven and on earth has been given to me" (Matt 28:18). The passive verb (has been given to me) is a so-called *passivum divinum*, a "divine passive." It indicates that God has now given *all authority, the fullness of power*, both *in heaven and on earth*, to his Son, who refused the offer of the tempter and followed the path of obedience (see Matt 3:15) and of suffering. The Son, who submitted to the Father, is set by the Father above all things. The closing promise, "behold, I am with you always, to the end of the age," reveals the qualitative difference between this power and the world dominion that was offered by the devil: the Son who has been installed as Lord of heaven and of earth remains united to his disciples. He does not sit on a throne above them as a potentate but is "in their midst" as their master (cf. Matt 18:20). In the Son, the divine power discloses itself as a power that brings benefits to others. This power that the Father bestows remains victorious. This is the answer that the Gospel, taken as a whole, gives to the devil.

The narrative of Jesus' disputation with the devil is a myth, and the farewell scene on the mountain at the end of the first Gospel at the very least makes use of mythical elements. This framework lifts the totality of Jesus' life above mere history and places it in the larger context of God's activity for the liberation of his people—indeed, of his whole creation. The juxtaposition of the two mountain scenes also shows clearly that the centrality of the question of power is in what the Gospels tell us about the life of Jesus, which lies between the two scenes. Two things become apparent.

First, power is not simply "power." There is a power of the devil, which violently subjects the other person to one's own will, and there is the power of the rule of God, which understands existence as coexistence[13] and hence acts not against the other but for him and with him.

Second, a struggle takes place between these two forms of power. This is depicted in various ways in the Gospels that interpret the life of Christ and in the Letters that interpret the life of Christians.

The present book seeks to investigate this conflict and to reflect on it. Our starting point is the differentiation in the idea of power, with regard to the (total) power of God in the first chapter and then with regard to the power of human beings in the following two chapters. The second chapter, with its starting point in the category of serving, which probably goes back to Jesus himself, looks at the use of power both within the Christian community and within the state. The third chapter takes its starting point in the Pauline category of humility and examines the attitude, the Christian "virtue," that lies behind this. A brief conclusion as a fourth chapter will then return one final time to the question of power.

This investigation will show that the Christ who provides orientation for Christian conduct is much more than a mere model for a Christian ethics. The earliest believers in Christ were convinced that Jesus' coming, and what God did through him and in him, had changed reality, and they expressed this conviction both in the christological hymns and formulae and in the account they gave of the story of

Jesus. Hidden in the lowliness of the crucified Jesus, the rule of God has dawned. A changeover of power has occurred through his exaltation, and the risen Jesus indicates this when he says that all power in heaven and on earth has been handed over to him. In their union with Christ, those who follow him already share in this new reality. This is why the Son of God becomes the archetype who leaves his mark on them: the new conduct of believers means that they "let themselves be borne" by the dynamism of the power of love that has been released upon the world in Christ and "get in tune" with this dynamism.[14] In this way, they are empowered not only to a future participation in his glory but also to a present-day participation in his gift of self.

Chapter 1

Power

Religion and Power: The Context in the History of Religion

It is not by chance that the devil begins with the title "Son of God," when he seeks to turn Jesus away from his path by seducing him to grasp a power that will be his own. The divine is always connected with power; indeed, divinity and power can almost become synonymous. U. von Wilamowitz-Moellendorff sums up the case of the Greek gods as follows: "The divine is that which is *kreitton* in relation to us. The gods are often called *kreittones*."[1] The comparative *kreitton* (more powerful) emphasizes the power of the gods. At the same time, the superior power is regarded as the decisive difference between the divine and the human; indeed, one might say that the superior power is divine. This does not only apply to the divine as an abstract; one particular deity can function as a predicate concept for power. For example, the name "Zeus" can denote not only the mythological ruler of the Olympian pantheon but also one particular form of divine power.[2] In one sense, therefore, we can say that the Greek deities are not so much persons as personifications of powers and that, consequently, Greek religion is concerned with the systematization of such powers.[3]

This immediate link between divinity and power is repeatedly made explicit in the ancient sources. The Attic poet Menander expresses it axiomatically: "everything that exercises power is called 'god.'"[4] In the Roman sphere, Cicero says something very similar in his treatise about the being of the gods: "whatever is outstanding is rightly adored."[5] A papyrus from the second century of the Common Era shows that this equation between divinity and power still held good in the imperial period. It begins with the question *[t]i theos?* (What does "god" mean?) and then gives the lapidary answer *t[o] kratoun* (the exercise of power).[6]

The link between power and religion is not restricted to the object of religious veneration. It also concerns the phenomenon of religion as such, inasmuch as this is always also a societal reality and is thus itself a factor of power. Religion justifies and legitimates rule and law in all the ancient cultures, and it regulates life in society. In the Roman Empire, for example, religion is so closely interwoven into every sphere of culture, of society, and especially of politics[7] that one can almost understand it as the ideological basis of Roman society and of the concept of the state,[8] and the regulations of religion can be described as sacral institutions.[9]

This bond between religion and political power found its most striking expression in the Roman imperial cult. As S. R. F. Price shows in his monograph *Rituals and Power*, one does not do justice to this phenomenon if one reduces it to a "religion of loyalty" that was instrumentalized by politics. The functionalization of the imperial cult in practical politics is undeniable; but it must be evaluated as an authentic religious phenomenon, which, precisely for this reason, plays a decisive role in the constitution of the power of the Roman imperial system.[10] In classical antiquity, therefore, "reflection on the gods" is always to be understood "also as a reflection on power"[11]—with all the attendant ambivalences.[12]

The Power of the God of Israel: Differentiations

At first sight, the biblical belief in God fits this pattern. The power to perform great miracles with his right hand and to annihilate his enemies is attributed to him as a complete matter of course (see Exod 15:6); and, as the Creator and sovereign Lord of the entire world, he possesses a unique power (see, in this regard, Pss 93–100). When the God of Israel is thus called "LORD Sabaoth," the "Lord of hosts," in the Old Testament, and this is rendered as *Kyrios pantokratôr*, "almighty Lord," in the Septuagint, the Greek translation of the Old Testament, the link between the idea of God and a power that is superior to everything else appears to have taken on a programmatic character. This does not remain restricted to the Old Testament. Christianity carries forward the Jewish inheritance in this area too, as we see not least from the fact that the only predicate of God that was included in the Apostolic Creed was his omnipotence—and not only once, but twice.[13]

At the same time, however, the Old Testament and early Jewish writings emphasize that the God who has liberated Israel and "cast Pharaoh's chariots and his army into the sea" (Exod 15:4) is *not* a God who is always "on the side of the big battalions."[14] As the one who breaks the bow of the strong and girds the weak with strength (cf. 1 Sam 2:4), God resists the arrogant power of human beings—and hence those who exalt themselves. This conviction finds its classic formulation in the Septuagint version of Proverbs 3:34:

> God resists the haughty,
> but he gives grace to the humble.[15]

It was not only in ancient Judaism that this antithetical *parallelismus membrorum* acquired the significance of a fundamental proposition about the relationship between God and human power;[16] this aphorism was profoundly influential in the New Testament and in early Christian literature as well,[17] and it played an important role not least in the elaboration of the ideal of humility (see below).

Parallels to the idea that the divinity raises up the lowly and brings down that which is high also exist outside the biblical tradition. It is precisely the link between an idea of the divine that has an increasingly ethical accentuation and the responsibility of God or the gods for justice that leads in the pagan sphere as well to a reluctance to associate earthly power unreflectingly with the divine. Hesiod already begins his *Works and Days* with a corresponding praise of Zeus:

> For easily he makes strong the weak,
> and easily he brings the strong man low;
> easily he humbles the proud and raises the obscure,
> and easily he straightens the crooked and blasts the proud—
> Zeus who thunders aloft and has his dwelling most high.[18]

The distinctiveness of the biblical testimony is that the God who cares for justice does not present himself as the one who "has his dwelling most high" above everything but as the one who decidedly takes the side of the weak. This other accent can be seen, for example, in the text that one could call the Old Testament counterpart to Hesiod's song in praise of Zeus, the song of Hannah, which in turn has its parallel in the New Testament in Mary's Magnificat (Luke 1:46-55):

> The bows of the mighty are broken,
> but the feeble gird on strength.
> Those who were full have hired themselves out for bread,
> but those who were hungry are fat with spoil. . . .
> The Lord kills and brings to life,

> he brings down to Sheol and raises up.
> The Lord makes poor and makes rich;
> he brings low, he also exalts.
> He raises up the poor from the dust;
> he lifts the needy from the ash heap,
> to make him sit with princes
> and inherit a seat of honor. (1 Sam 2:4-8)

In keeping with this, Psalm 113 sees the very point of God's being enthroned on high in his bending down into the depths and thus raising up the one who is lowly:

> He is seated on high,
> he looks far down
> on the heavens and the earth.
> He raises the poor from the dust,
> and lifts the needy from the ash heap,
> to make him sit with princes,
> with the princes of his people. (113:5-8)

"The Lord is my strength"

This is not the expression of an arbitrary partisanship. Rather, this turning to the lowly expresses a specific understanding of divine power, which may perhaps not be unique in the history of religion, but which comes into its own in a particularly pregnant manner in the biblical writings. For, despite all the emphasis on God's preeminence, his greatness does not consist in the *kreitton*, his superior power, and thus not in his difference from the weakness of the human person. Instead, God's power benefits his human partner. Indeed, it becomes his own power, and the psalmist who experiences oppression can praise his God as his strength:

> I love you, O Lord, my strength.
> The Lord is my rock, my fortress, and my deliverer. (Ps 18:2-3)

In another Psalm, the one who prays professes his belief:

> The Lord is my light and my salvation;
> whom shall I fear?
> The Lord is the stronghold of my life;
> of whom shall I be afraid? (27:1)

This praise is often summed up in the pregnant formula: "the Lord is my strength" (Hab 3:19; cf. Pss 43:2; 46:2; 59:18; 81:2; et passim). "Decisive is the soteriological relational aspect of Yahweh's power."[19] Psalm 62:12-13 expresses this with a synthetic *parallelismus membrorum* in which the second part tellingly switches from an impersonal statement to a direct address:

> Power belongs to God,
> and steadfast love belongs to you, O Lord.

The counterpart of this God, whose sovereignty consists in his exaltation of the one who is lowly, is the human being who does not want to amount to anything in his own right but awaits everything from God. It is not always easy here to distinguish clearly between a lowly situation in which the believer finds himself because of external circumstances and a lowliness that is the attitude whereby the believer foregoes arrogance. These two already overlap in the Old Testament and in Judaism, and this is well illustrated in the New Testament by a comparison of the Matthean Sermon on the Mount with the Lukan Sermon on the Plain, where the beatitude pronounced on the materially poor at Luke 6:20, which is probably more original, becomes the beatitude pronounced on the "poor in spirit" in Matthew 5:3. But irrespective of whether this is a situation or an attitude, fellowship with God is promised not to those on high but to those below:

> The Lord is near to the brokenhearted,
> and saves the crushed in spirit.[20] (Ps 34:19)

This different understanding of God thus implies a different ideal human being: in the Bible, it is not the human being who himself strives for higher things who becomes the counterpart of God, but the one who knows that he is distinct from God and dependent upon him and who thus corresponds to the divine will to enter into a relationship. Accordingly, even a "humiliation" can become the occasion for praise and thanksgiving, since it has led the believer to throw himself unconditionally into the arms of this God (see Ps 119:67, 71). This will later become significant with regard to the consequences for human conduct; at this point, it is first of all important to note, with regard to God, that the power of the biblical God is linked ever more closely to his will to enter into a relationship. This becomes especially clear in the divine predicate, which, we are often told, expresses most directly the boundless superior power of God, namely, his omnipotence.

From Yahweh Zebaoth to the Almighty

In those parts of the Septuagint that are translated from Hebrew, with the exception of the book of Job, *Pantokratôr* is almost always employed together with *Kyrios* as a translation of *Yhwh Ṣĕbā'ôt*. In these passages, *Pantokratôr* is an addition that defines the divine name *Yhwh/Kurios* more precisely, but it is increasingly employed absolutely in Hellenistic Judaism. *Pantokratôr* (the Almighty) becomes a distinct name for God.[21] This, however, does not mean that the idea of power becomes the interpreter of the idea of God. In fact, the opposite seems to be the case, since there is at the same time an ever-stronger emphasis in the early Jewish texts that the God who is called King, Lord, Ruler, or Almighty is and remains the God of Israel,[22] whose power benefits his people.[23] It is above all in the context of oppression by enemies and of the violence suffered by Israel that the Almighty is invoked, praised, and attested as the Savior of his people. One characteristic example is the speech in which Judas Maccabeus encourages his soldiers to fight:

> They trust to arms and acts of daring,
> but we trust in the Almighty God,
> who is able with a single nod
> to strike down those who are coming against us,
> and even, if necessary, the whole world. (2 Macc 8:18)

A fine example in the area of the divine predicates is the book of Judith, which was probably written in the second or first century before the Common Era.[24] It repeatedly speaks of "the Almighty" (Jdt 4:13; 8:13; 15:10; 16:6, 17), but it also professes faith in God as a "God of the lowly, helper of the oppressed, upholder of the weak, protector of the forsaken, savior of those without hope" (Jdt 9:11; cf. 4:9; 6:19).[25] It thus remains decisive for the understanding of the Jewish God that his power is no *potentia absoluta*, but a *potentia personalis sive relationis*.[26]

This soteriological qualification of the idea of omnipotence is not without support in the Greek term that is employed for omnipotence in the biblical-Jewish tradition. *Pantokratôr* is a so-called *nomen actionis*. This noun may in fact have been coined within Judaism; at any rate, it was decisively influenced by Judaism.[27] Unlike the adjective *pankratês*, which is occasionally found in pagan texts as a divine predicate[28] and to which the Latin *omnipotens* and the English "almighty" correspond, the word *pantokratôr* is not exclusively associated semantically with the concept of dominance. The verb *kratein* also means "to hold in the hand" and "to make good."[29] In Latin patristic authors, *pantokratôr* is translated not only by *omnipotens* (almighty) but also by *omnitenens* (holding everything), a word that is not attested in profane Latin literature and was probably coined by the Christians specifically as a translation of *pantokratôr*.[30] We find something similar in the Syriac translation, which consistently renders the New Testament concept as *hū d'ahid kul*, "who holds everything." Accordingly, *pantokratôr* should be understood in the sense of the spiritual "he's got the whole world in his hand," which praises God's power as a place of refuge for the powerless.

The Son of God and the Rule of God: God's (Total) Power in the Gospels

When Jesus proclaims the dawning of the rule of God and calls this his Gospel, his good news (Mark 1:14-15 par.), the idea of divine power in his message is virtually identical with salvation. The kingdom of God is the rule of the Father who conceals himself from the wise and understanding but reveals himself in his Son to infants (Matt 11:25 par. Luke 10:21). This revelation is hidden under its opposite—*sub contrario*, as the Reformers called it—because it comes to the world in the lowly form of a Galilean carpenter whose earthly life ends on the cross.

This further intensifies the idea of the divine power as the power that God shares. For example, in the prehistory of the Gospel of Luke, Mary "exalts" (Latin: *magnificat*) the greatness of God, who has "looked on the lowliness of his maidservant" (Luke 1:48).[31] She praises him as the "Mighty one," because he has "thrust down the mighty ones from their thrones" (1:52). This God is the "Most High" (1:32, 35) because he "has lifted up the lowly" (1:52, cf. 14:11; 18:14). The archangel says that nothing is impossible for God (cf. 1:37); and, through this reversal of existing power structures and the share that he thereby gives in his own glory and power, he has shown that he is the Savior (1:47) and is merciful (1:50, 54).

The Son of God in the Gospels lives out of trust in the power of the Creator and sustainer whose throne is the sky and whose footstool is the earth (Matt 5:34-35), who makes his sun rise and rain fall (Matt 5:45) and thus cares for his creation and sustains it, even down to the lilies of the field and the birds of the air (Matt 6:26ff. par. Luke 12:22ff.). This trust generates his certainty that the Creator, who even now preserves and sustains life, will not let the powers of destruction, of sickness, of evil, and of death, which are at work in the creation at present, have the last word. Rather, the Creator is even now establishing his rule in the creation, beginning with Jesus' activity,[32] and this is why he will ultimately bring about redemption.[33] The actions that are known as Jesus' miracles denote the appearing of the redemption that is the result of God's entering upon his rule. It is significant that these are not called miracles in the Gospels. The Greek word for this would be *thaumata*, a miraculous breaking of the laws of nature that cause *thaumazein*, "admiration" of the wonder worker; but Jesus' wonders are called *dunameis*, "deeds of power," because they are concerned with making the creation whole. This takes place when the destructive forces are stripped of their power through God's mighty working in Jesus (cf. Mark 3:23-27 par.; Acts 10:38).

This explains Jesus' categorical refusal to perform miracles as an accreditation, despite the repeated demands of both his enemies and his admirers.[34] He has already made it clear, in the temptation narrative, that power for its own sake is diabolical. Just as the reference to the Father as the source of power is constitutive of the concept of *exousia* (authority, full power), so too Jesus' mighty deeds turn the spotlight not on him but on God, in whose name he acts.[35] The mighty deeds benefit those who are weak and need care and assistance, the sick and those possessed by evil spirits. The power of the rule of God is revealed in Jesus' activity as a countervailing power against the powers that destroy life. In Jesus' authoritative actions against sickness, hunger, and possession, in Jesus' authoritative teaching against lovelessness, delusion, and greed, his authority is always a power that heals and helps. It is in this sense that his proclamation of the dawning rule of God is "Gospel," the good news that he addresses to those in need. In keeping with this, the evangelist Luke "translates" the proclamation of the dawning rule of God in Mark into the first sermon in Nazareth, where the Lukan Jesus sees the predictions of the prophets as already fulfilled through and in himself "today":[36]

> The Spirit of the Lord is upon me,
> because he has anointed me
> to bring good news to the poor.
> He has sent me to proclaim release to the captives
> and recovery of sight to the blind,
> to let the oppressed go free,
> to proclaim the year of the Lord's favor. (Luke 4:18-19)

This sounds more harmless than it in fact is, since we must not overlook the point that these words pose a fundamental question to other forms of power,[37] both the exercise of power in religion and the usurpation of religion to serve power. Accordingly, Jesus' whole life is permeated by disputations that reflect this conflict with those who imagine that God is on their side. The conflict reaches its high point in the passion, and it is noteworthy that precisely here, where the action of making present the rule of God leads to the powerlessness of the Son of God, Jesus himself not only holds fast to the conviction of God's power but actually emphasizes it all the more decisively. It is significant that the Son of God does not call upon his Father as the "Almighty" in the days of his mighty wonders but precisely in the night of the deepest contestation, in Gethsemane: "Abba, Father, for you all things are possible" (Mark 14:36). Jesus speaks not only of God's rule but of his omnipotence, precisely where God is hidden, where there is no answer to the threefold prayer of his Son, whose soul is troubled even unto death, that the chalice may pass him by. "For you all things are possible": this is the trusting anticipation of what God, as the Father, can make possible.[38] In the midst of his own powerlessness, Jesus holds fast so decisively to the counterfactual saving power of his Father that he can address the Sanhedrin and tell the judges who condemn him that their triumph will not be definitive: instead, he himself will be "seated at the right hand of the power" (i.e., of God) and will come "with the clouds of heaven" (Mark 14:62).

The Gospels attest that, since this trust is confirmed by the Father in the resurrection, the suffering and dying of the Son of Man who is handed over to his enemies do not refute of his message about the rule of God that has drawn near. Rather, his suffering and dying bring the covenant into effect (Mark 14:24 par. Matt 26:28) or establish the new covenant (Luke 22:20; cf. 1 Cor 11:25). This is why the passion is not passed over in silence when the story of Jesus' life is told in the Gospel. On the contrary, it is the vanishing point of the whole story. This "divine" dimension behind the earthly events is already presented in the oldest Gospel, in the transfiguration narrative (Mark 9:2ff.), which follows the first prediction of Jesus' suffering and not only repeats but actually intensifies the assurance at the beginning of the Gospel that Jesus is the Son of God: the Son of Man who is going to his death is proleptically transformed into a heavenly figure. Similarly, it is the centurion under the cross (of all people) who confesses Jesus as the "Son of God" immediately after his death (Mark 15:39 par.).

The other two synoptic evangelists also depict this changeover of power, each in his own way: in Matthew, through the scene on the mountain, mentioned above, in which the risen Jesus, who has been appointed Lord over heaven and earth, assures the disciples that he will always remain with them (Matt 28:18-20), and in Luke, through the ascension that allows Jesus to equip his followers with "power from on high" (Luke 24:49; cf. Acts 1:8; 2:33).

God's Empowering Power in Paul

Paul too can interpret the death and the resurrection of Jesus as a changeover of power: it is here that death begins to be stripped of its power.[39] In his theology of the cross, the apostle, more acutely than any other New Testament writer, thinks through the consequences of the death and resurrection for the idea of power, too. He writes in the First Letter to the Corinthians:

> For the message about the cross is foolishness to those who are perishing but to us who are being saved it is the power of God. . . .
> For Jews demand signs and Greeks desire wisdom,
> but we proclaim Christ crucified,
> a stumbling block to Jews and foolishness to Gentiles,
> but to those who are the called, both Jews and Greeks,
> Christ the power of God and the wisdom of God.
> For God's foolishness is wiser than human [wisdom],
> and God's weakness is stronger than human [strength].
> (1 Cor 1:18, 22-25)

The apparently paradoxical affirmation that "God's weakness" proves itself to be stronger than the strength of human beings is no mere assertion in Paul. This interpretation of the Christ event is for him the quintessence of his experience of God, which is defined by the cross. The God who has appointed Christ in the resurrection to be Lord over the dead and the living (Rom 14:9) is the basis of the hope that Paul proclaims, namely, that what is now sown in transience, dishonor, and weakness will one day be raised up by God in permanence, glory, and power (1 Cor 15:42). The God "who gives life to the dead and calls into existence the things that do not exist" (Rom 4:17) reveals himself already in the present life of the believers as the one who overcomes lowliness and weakness, so that those who are "in Christ Jesus" are now "dead to sin and alive to God" (Rom 6:11). This allows the apostle to make his *theologia crucis* plausible to the Corinthians by means of a reference to their own calling into the fellowship of salvation:[40]

> Consider your own call, brothers and sisters:
> not many of you were wise by human standards,
> not many were powerful,
> not many were of noble birth.
> But God chose what is foolish in the world to shame the wise;
> God chose what is weak in the world to shame the strong;
> God chose what is low and despised in the world,
> things that are not,
> to reduce to nothing things that are. (1 Cor 1:26-28)

This finds even stronger expression in the Second Letter to the Corinthians, once again in view of what he himself, as an apostle, has experienced of God. He has already described God at the beginning of this Letter as the power of life that overcomes death, a power that takes effect in him both as preservation and as rescue (2 Cor 1:8-11), and as a revitalization of the inner person in the midst of the decay of his external existence:

> But we have this treasure in clay jars,
> so that it may be made clear
> that this extraordinary power belongs to God and not to us.
> We are afflicted in every way, but not crushed;
> perplexed, but not driven to despair;
> persecuted, but not forsaken;
> struck down, but not destroyed,
> always carrying in the body the death of Jesus,
> so that the life of Jesus may also be made visible in our
> bodies. . . .
> So we do not lose heart.
> Even though our outer nature is wasting away,
> our inner nature is being renewed day by day.
> (2 Cor 4:7-10, 16)

The entire existence of the apostle is determined by the revelation of the power of God in lowliness and powerlessness, the "new creation in Christ" (2 Cor 5:17; cf. 6:3-10).

The empowering character of the divine power in powerlessness is set out above all in the so-called foolish speech in 2 Corinthians 11–12, where Paul offers a kind of summary of his own life from the perspective of the power of God that reveals itself in the cross. These remarks are occasioned by the accusations by other apostles who have made their way into the community and allege that Paul's authorization as an apostle of Christ cannot be verified by means of an imposing public appearance and extraordinary experiences.[41] His opponents argue, in a way that recalls the tempter in the story of Jesus (Matt 4:1-11 par. Luke 4:1-13), that something extraordinary ought to be perceptible in the public appearance of one who has God to back him up;[42] and it is clear that this argument has won over many members of the community. The apostle, who is being pushed out of his own community, is in a dilemma: on the one hand, he wants to win back his community to himself and to his message, but, on the other hand, he does not want to engage with his opponents in a contest of self-praise, since that would be an admission that they were substantially correct—and that, in turn, would give the lie to his theology of the cross. Paul resolves the dilemma with a rhetorical masterpiece, the "foolish speech,"[43] in which he repeatedly hints that he too could present impressive deeds of power and experiences. At the same time, however, he emphasizes that all showmanship of this kind, far from benefiting the community, would ultimately militate against its upbuilding. In the First Letter to the Corinthians, Paul likes to call this "puffing oneself up." All it does is demonstrate to other people that they are inferior, thus destroying the fellowship. But it is precisely the apostle's own weakness that makes him sensitive to the weaknesses of the others:

> Who is weak, and I am not weak?
> Who is made to stumble, and I am not indignant?
> (2 Cor 11:29)

It is this sensitivity, a readiness to share in others' suffering that is necessarily accompanied by vulnerability, that has empowered the apostle to address an astonishingly large number of women and men with his message and to integrate them into the community, so that they actively support him as fellow workers in his worldwide mission.[44] But the question of weakness and strength concerns not only the "horizontal" relationship to one's neighbor, but also the "vertical" relationship to God, since "puffing oneself up" not only marginalizes one's fellow human beings but also leaves no space for God, who thus cannot fill the human being with his power. The mystery of the cross is that in it, as Paul says at 1 Corinthians 1:25, the weakness of God proves to be stronger than the strength of human beings. Accordingly, the apostle does not conclude his "foolish speech" with the things of which he could boast in the eyes of the Corinthians—not with his miracles that he has worked among them and to which the community can testify (2 Cor 12:12; cf. Rom 15:19) nor with his vision of Christ, to which he alludes, but for which he consciously substitutes a very different Damascus experience, his risky flight from King Aretas (2 Cor 11:32-33). He even puts a distance between himself and his journey to heaven, which took him as far as the third paradise (2 Cor 12:3-4) by speaking of it only in the third person. Instead, he concludes his speech provocatively with the antihistory[45] of a failure. As with Jesus in Gethsemane before him, here too there is a threefold prayer that is not heard: the prayer to be freed from an illness that the apostle calls the "thorn in the flesh" (2 Cor 12:7). Paul can present this defeat as something advantageous to him because Christ himself has commented on the rejection of his request with the assurance of his powerful presence precisely in the apostle's weakness:

> My grace is sufficient for you,
> for power is made perfect in weakness. (2 Cor 12:9a)

There is thus no contradiction between weakness and the presence of God. Rather, weakness is the place in which the divine power unfolds in the apostle. In this way, something that initially appears to confirm the reproach of a weak spirituality on the part of the apostle becomes the proof of a strength that comes from the union with his exalted Lord.[46] Paul can thus draw the conclusion:

> So I will boast all the more gladly of my weaknesses,
> so that the power of Christ may dwell in me. (2 Cor 12:9b)

His final inference is at first sight paradoxical: "For whenever I am weak, then I am strong" (2 Cor 12:10). Through his own example, the apostle shows that vulnerability and suffering are not simply identical with powerlessness but, thanks to fellowship with Christ, God's power can be at work in them with the "weapons of our warfare, which are not merely of the flesh, but have divine power to destroy strongholds" (2 Cor 10:4). This power was bestowed by the Lord not in order to tear down the community but to build it up (2 Cor 10:8). This is why this power does not separate the apostle from the community but unites him to it.

Since this can easily be misunderstood, let me once again emphasize that, when Paul speaks in this way of God's power, he is not making a virtue out of necessity, since it is precisely in his situation of bodily decrepitude and external powerlessness that he can point to an immense success in his mission. When he writes the Second Letter to the Corinthians, he is on the point of subjugating the Roman Empire from east to west—in the opposite direction to its original expansion, as it were—to his crucified Lord,

> by the power [*en dunamei*] of signs and wonders,
> by the power [*en dunamei*] of the Spirit of God. (Rom 15:19)

According to 2 Corinthians 10:12-16, this is the letter of recommendation of his apostleship that Paul himself does not write: it comes from God. The power of the Gospel, which renews him again and again even in the midst of external decay (2 Cor 4:7-18), is not a "fleshly" power (2 Cor 10:3) that is under his control but a spiritual power that is bestowed by God. "The Spirit helps us in our weakness," as the apostle says in Romans 8:26, or, as he writes at Galatians 3:5,

> [God] supplies you with the Spirit
> and works miracles among you.

Even when he is weary of the struggle (Phil 1:23) and sits in prison, externally powerless (Phil 1:13-14), the apostle can still make the following provocative formulation: "I can do all things through him who strengthens me" (Phil 4:13). This experience of an empowering power of God was so fundamental for the apostle that he coins a specific word for it, which is virtually unattested in Greek hitherto:[47] *endunamoun*, "to impart or instill strength."[48] This idea, under the slogan of "empowerment,"[49] has made its way via American community psychology into modern concepts of management and social help.[50] But power of this kind always remains the power of the cross. In other words, it is not a magic potion that turns the believer into a superman, and it is more than a "soft skill" for dealing with one's employees. Rather, this is a power that is the fruit of participation in the lowliness and suffering of Christ. It is there that a spiritual strength grows for the apostle that makes him strong in his weakness—to the benefit of others.

Empowerment in the Pauline School

The apostle's pupils—or those who see themselves as standing in his tradition and therefore write under his name—take up the verb *endunamoun* and the idea of the empowering power. At 1 Timothy 1:12, "Paul" thanks Christ "who has strengthened me," and a similar statement is found at 2 Timothy 4:17. This applies also to his fellow workers: in 2 Timothy 2:1, the fictive Paul exhorts his "son" Timothy to become strong through the grace that is in Christ.

The idea of the divine empowering is translated into the life of the believers in a particularly striking way in Ephesians 6:10-17. The beginning of the Letter to the Ephesians states that God has already let "the immeasurable greatness of his power" become operative in the Christians (1:19)—the same power through which he raised up Christ and "seated him at his right hand in the heavenly places, far above all rule and authority and power and dominion" (1:20). The Pauline idea that the believers are citizens of heaven (Phil 3:20; Gal 4:26) is referred here, much more explicitly than by the apostle himself, to the church as the all-embracing sphere where the Kyrios rules (see above; Eph 2:1-3, 7; 4:1-16). In its closing paraenesis, the Letter to the Ephesians borrows Pauline metaphors that speak of putting on "the armor of light" (Rom 13:12) or "the breastplate of faith" and "the helmet of hope" (1 Thess 5:8), and it outlines the allegory of a spiritual "whole body armor" of Christians that equips them with the divine weapons of defense for their fight

> against the rulers,
> against the authorities,
> against the cosmic powers of this present darkness,
> against the spiritual forces of evil in the heavenly places.
> (Eph 6:12)

This passage begins with the exhortation to the readers to let themselves be equipped with God's power:

> Finally, let yourselves be empowered [*endunamousthe*]
> in the Lord
> and in the strength of his power.
> Put on the whole armor of God. (6:10-11)

The Almighty in the Revelation of John

Although the New Testament leaves no doubt that God is able to do what he plans to do, it is strikingly reticent about applying predicates of power to God. This is most likely connected with the special character of the empowering, "spiritual" power of God. Jesus proclaims the kingly rule of God, but he calls God "Father," not "King." He emphasizes that God can do all things, but he does not speak of the "Almighty." Similarly, Paul defines the Gospel as the "power of God" (*dunamis theou*) and expects that God will finally be all in all (1 Cor 15:28), but he usually refrains from applying one of the otherwise customary predicates of power to God. These predicates are either completely absent from the New Testament (such as *monarkhos*), or else very rare (*despotês, dunatos, hupsistos*). Even *Kyrios*, the translation of God's name in the Old Testament, is used of God mostly in Old Testament quotations and allusions; in roughly two-thirds of its occurrences, it is transferred to Christ. The hymn in the Letter to the Philippians praises this transfer as the consequence of the obedient self-emptying of Christ.[51]

Despite their firm belief and hope in God's ability to act, therefore, the New Testament authors clearly avoided too direct a link between God and power, probably because they wanted to prevent the divine from being misunderstood as the tempter misunderstood it, namely, as a predicate concept for superior power. This is why the predicate of omnipotence is found nowhere in the Gospels and only once in Paul.[52] There is, however, one striking exception to this rule: the last book of the Bible, which is the only surviving writing by an early Christian prophet, the Revelation of John.

The seer understands the experience of oppression by Rome, the "harlot Babylon, drunk with the blood of the saints" (Rev 17:1-6), as the beginning of a Satanic attempt at extermination. This leads him to contrast God's power with the apparently omnipotent *Imperium Romanum* and hence to invoke, confess, and praise God throughout the entire book as the "Almighty." The author experiences the Roman Empire as violent, and he counters it with the power of God, which is presented as an opposing power. The result, especially in the cycles of visions, is that the power of God takes on strongly violent traits, in the style of pertinent earlier texts from the Old Testament prophecies of judgment.

When we look more closely, however, we see that even in this book—which can be understood appropriately only as an extreme response to an extreme situation—the seer is certainly aware of the otherness of the divine power, and he does not fail to make this point. In the opening vision (Rev 4:1–5:14), it is significant that it is not the mighty dwellers in heaven who are able to open the book with the seven seals and thus initiate the redemption of the world, but the slain Lamb (Rev 5:6). The disruption in the metaphors is eloquent. The "lion of the tribe of Judah" is announced (5:5), but the savior who brings victory over the powers of death is not the beast of prey that lives from the lives of others but the sacrificial animal that has given its life for the others.[53] In keeping with this, the ultimate goal of all the terrors of the cycles of vision is "to destroy those who destroy the earth" (Rev 11:18), so that at the end a new heaven and a new earth can come (Rev 21:1-4), where God wipes away all tears (Rev 7:17; 21:4) and destroys death (Rev 20:14; 21:4), so that death and cries will be no more (Rev 21:4).

The New Testament as a Power Struggle

Our examination of the New Testament writings has shown that the power of God is a counterfactual element there, perhaps even more clearly than in the Old Testament. It is God's (total) power that Jesus calls "Abba, Father" (Mark 14:36). Since this God, through the Son, becomes the Father of the disciples too (Matt 6:9; Luke 11:2; cf. Gal 4:6; Rom 8:15), the name of "Father" increasingly complements and replaces the appellation *theos* (God). God's will to enter into relationship, which is expressed in this new name, determines the understanding of God and hence also the understanding of his power. The creed does justice to this by subordinating the predicate of omnipotence to the name of "Father." This, however, means (to put it in somewhat simplistic terms) that the biblical God is not a predicate concept of power. Rather, the (total) power is an attribute of his fatherhood.

This means that the relationship between God and power becomes dialectical, as we saw in our exposition of the temptation narrative. The New Testament holds decidedly fast to the power of the heavenly Father, but at the same time, this constitutes a contradiction of other conceptions of power and thereby makes necessary a differentiation in the concept of power. A concept of the divine (total) power that is in conformity with the Gospel cannot be a religious elevation of mere force; the "Almighty" is not the superlative form of an absolutist ruler. Rather, the entire New Testament must be read as the drama of a power struggle between two opposed forms of power: the force used on one's own authority with the goal of subjugating others, and the spiritual power that is generated by union with God and finds expression in taking care of others and in fellowship.[54] Or, to put it in the words that Jesus himself uses when he makes a differentiation in the concept of power, oppression is the opposite of the authority of the one who is the first precisely as the servant and slave of all.

In the Pauline and Johannine traditions, therefore, it is *love* that is associated with God and hence also with his power. And this means that love struggles against everything that still seeks to dominate the believers. Paul expresses this conflict by speaking of the antithesis between grace and law and between righteousness and sin, and in the believers and especially in the mutual antagonism of spirit and flesh:

> For what the flesh desires is opposed to the spirit,
> and what the spirit desires is opposed to the flesh;
> for these are opposed to each other,
> to prevent you from doing what you want. (Gal 5:17)

The Gospel of John is shaped by the corresponding antitheses between light and darkness, death and life, and falsehood and truth.

The New Testament writers are convinced that this conflict has already been resolved in principle through the death and resurrection of Jesus Christ: "nothing can any longer separate" the believers "from the love of God in Christ Jesus," which is stronger than every other power, including death (Rom 8:38-39). And this means that grace has already displaced as ruler the sin that dominates the world through death (Rom 5:21). "Take courage! I have conquered the cosmos!"—this is how the same conviction is expressed by means of a resultative perfect on the lips of the Johannine Christ (John 16:33). Similarly, the First Letter of John says that everyone who loves is born of God, because God is love (4:7-8) and that the one who is born of God conquers the world (5:4).

The love that "bears all things" (1 Cor 13:7) is wonderful as a power that preserves and maintains, a power that makes the gift of self, a power that has compassion for the guilty and the weak and therefore gives weakness a helping hand; but it is also vulnerable. It is not the power that announces its presence as destruction. It is the unobtrusive care through which the Creator preserves this world as a place of life and the Redeemer leads it to its consummation as a new creation. In short, it is a serving power.

Is this power omnipotent? That is, of course, something that can only be an object of our belief, which is based on the conquering of death at Easter; for as Galatians 5:17 says, the power struggle that is already resolved in Jesus is still taking place in the believers, insofar as they still live "in the flesh." And their hope in the consummation of the world, when "God is all in all" (1 Cor 15:28), must stand the test at present in a struggle that is waged with God's help against all the antagonistic powers (see Eph 6:12).

Since faith expresses itself vis-à-vis one's fellow human being in love (see Gal 5:6), the whole of the believing existence, including the way we deal with power, must be in accord with God's will to enter into relationship. The empowering, "serving power" thus becomes the criterion for the human use of power. And this brings us to the next chapter.

Chapter 2

Service

Attachment between Enslavement and Liberation
Differentiations in the Idea of Service

The New Testament presupposes that the human being always exists in relationships. The human being is integrated into relationships, and they orient him and define him. This dependence is often called service. In this sense, for example, the verb *douleuô* denotes "an obligation to service and a readiness to service"[1] that constitute the human being as such and have nothing per se to do with the freedom or lack of freedom of the human person. Freedom and the lack of freedom are determined not by the fact of serving but by the question, "To whom or to what is the one who serves subordinate, or does one subordinate oneself?" There are realities that bring the human being into dependence and thus into a lack of freedom. In the Letter to the Galatians, the apostle identifies the powers of the cosmos (Gal 4:3) and the gods that by nature are no gods (Gal 4:8) as spheres of power under which the believers were enslaved in the past.

In the Letter to the Romans, Paul mentions especially the sin that dominates the human being and makes him its slave (Rom 5:21).

It is, however, significant that this kind of dependence is spoken about from the perspective of the believers looking back at their former lives. They are indeed still warned against this dependence, since believers are continually threatened by the possibility of relapse. But the important point is that it is only on the basis of liberation in Christ that the earlier allegiances can be perceived as a bondage that made them slaves.[2] The Gospel is presented, in contrast to this lack of freedom, as a countervailing power that sets free. For example, Paul says in Romans 6:6 that

> our old self was crucified with [Christ]
> so that the body of sin might be destroyed,
> and we might no longer serve sin.

When the apostle then goes on to repeat this assurance in the form of a demand that sin should no longer be allowed to rule in one's body and that the members of the body should be made available to God as weapons of righteousness (Rom 6:12-13), he makes it clear that liberation through Christ does not lead to human autonomy. As a liberation that is generated by union with God or with Christ, it is the result of a new bond that can also be called a service. Now, however, this is a service that is to be rendered to God or to the Lord:[3]

> For just as you once presented your members
> to impurity and to greater and greater iniquity,
> so now present your members
> as slaves to righteousness for sanctification. (Rom 6:19)

Service of this kind is

> serving in the new way of the Spirit
> and not in the old way of the letter. (Rom 7:6)

Service as Freedom

"Service" is thus not a univocal term. On the one hand, there is a "yoke" of slavery to the entities that, as "powers of the cosmos," enslave the human being (Gal 4:3) and take him captive through "the law of sin that dwells in my members" (Rom 7:23). And on the other hand, there is the bond to God that shelters believers in God's loving care and thus—in accordance with God's power, which does not deprive its partner of power but empowers him[4]—liberates them through the Spirit to become children of God:

> So you are no longer a slave, but a son,
> and if a son, then also an heir, through God.
> (Gal 4:7; cf. Rom 8:14-17)

Whether serving is a heteronomy that enslaves or something that liberates to self-determination depends on the lord in question. A liberating service is possible where, as a "freedman of the Lord," one submits totally to the "Lord" Jesus Christ as his slave, instead of being "slaves of human beings" (1 Cor 7:22-23). This explains Paul's apparently paradoxical statement that believers, who were slaves of sin (Rom 6:17), have now been set free—liberated to become "slaves of righteousness":

> Having been set free from sin,
> you have become slaves of righteousness. (Rom 6:18)

It is in this sense that the paraenesis of the First Letter of Peter can equate freedom with dependence on God, when it exhorts its addressees:

> Live as free people,
> yet do not use your freedom as a pretext for evil—
> but as slaves of God. (1 Pet 2:16)

In the epistolary literature, the term "servant" or "slave" of God is the honorable name of the children of God—and at the same time their obligation, as "children of obedience" (1 Pet 1:14), to preserve their freedom in the allegiance to Christ or to God. We find something comparable in the Jesus tradition. The so-called Logia source transmits a logion in which Jesus demands of those who follow him that they take a decision about the "Lord" to whom they wish to submit:

> No one can serve two masters;
> for he will either hate the one and love the other,
> or be devoted to the one and despise the other.
> You cannot serve God and Mammon!
> (Matt 6:24 par. Luke 16:13)

Accordingly, a few verses after Paul has said that the old human being has been crucified with Christ so that he no longer serves sin (Rom 6:6), he can repeat this as a demand:

> Therefore, do not let sin exercise dominion in your mortal bodies,
> to make you obey their passions.[5] (Rom 6:12)

The service of God "in the new way of the Spirit" has one further addressee: one who stands before God is at the same time set under his fellow human beings. In other words, the freedom bestowed by God is also put into effect in the service of one's neighbor (1 Cor 7:19; Gal 5:13).[6] With regard to such a service, we must draw a further distinction between a direct and an indirect service. The direct service is service in the Christian community, where dealings with one another find their orientation in the life of Jesus and a life which is defined by his gift of self in such a way that the totality of ethics can be summarized in the requirement of mutual service—a requirement that is further intensified with regard to the church ministries, that is to say, with regard to power. But it is not only the office bearer in the Christian community who is a servant of God. The same is true of one who holds office in the state (and, at the time of Paul, all of these were pagans). According to Paul, he too "bears the sword" as the servant of God, since it is he who maintains, by force if need be, the ordering that is necessary for life in society in this world. In this way, he indirectly implements the will of God. Let us begin by looking at direct service.

The Service of Christ and the Serving of Christians in the Gospels

In all four Gospels, when it is a question of power, the dealings of Christians with one another are explicitly or implicitly seen in relation to the obligating figure of the serving Lord. In Mark, the oldest Gospel, which is shaped by the evangelist's theology of the passion, this relation of the Christian ethics to the passion of Christ is formulated as part of the instruction that Jesus gives his disciples on the way to Jerusalem. The evangelist forms Jesus' path into suffering as a loosely linked itinerary from Caesarea Philippi in the north to Jerusalem in the south. It is given its structure by means of three predictions (Mark 8:31; 9:31; 10:32-33) in which Jesus announces his suffering and his resurrection as the destiny envisaged by God for him.[7] Such a suffering of extreme violence seems a dramatic contradiction of the proclamation of the dawning rule of God, which has characterized Jesus' public activity and his mission up to this point (Mark 1:14-15). At the first prediction, therefore, Peter—who has just been the first to confess Jesus as the Messiah—threatens his master (Mark 8:32) to deter him from taking the path of suffering (cf. Matt 16:22). Jesus then rebuffs him as "Satan," because his human ideas contradict the plans of God (Mark 8:33 par.). This rebuff indicates that here, as in the temptation narrative from the Logia source that we discussed in the prelude, the fundamental issue is the correct understanding of Jesus' task and of the authority that is linked to this task. The starting point in both instances is the christological titles of sovereignty: in the temptation narrative, the "Son of God," and here, the "Christ/Messiah." In both instances, the interpretation of the title is presented as a decision for God or for Satan, but here it is no longer a question of the decision to be taken by the Son of God but of the decision to be taken by those who follow him.

The harshness of this rebuff of Peter—the disciple who features most prominently alongside Jesus in the Gospels—is unparalleled, but it has no lasting effect on the disciples. According to the account in the oldest Gospel, they have nothing better to do after the second prediction of Jesus' suffering than to quarrel along the way about which of them is the greatest. In his reply, Jesus makes power his theme for the first time,[8] and he makes it clear that, while the hierarchy of above and below is not abolished for those who follow him, the justification for such a hierarchy is turned upside down:[9]

> Whoever wants to be first
> must be last of all and servant of all. (Mark 9:35)

But even with these words, he seems to achieve nothing. The *libido dominandi*, the urge to put oneself in the limelight and to acquire superior power, proves stronger, and there is yet another conflict in the context of Jesus' announcement of his future suffering. This time, Jesus redefines the disciples' relationship to power on the basis of the gift he makes of his own life. The starting point, immediately after the third prediction of suffering in Mark 10:32-33, is the request of the sons of Zebedee, James and John, to sit one day at his right hand and at his left. This request by the two disciples, who are, with Peter, Jesus' closest confidants (cf. Mark 5:37; 9:2; 14:33), is not in the least the fruit of a moving desire for personal closeness.[10] The addition of "in your glory" shows that the sons of Zebedee want to sit with Jesus on the throne. In other words, they want to rule and judge at his side.

The dialogue that follows this request is given an unusual structure by Jesus' double answer.[11] Whatever the reason for the striking doubling of question and answer may be,[12] this whole dialogue now forms the beginning of a lengthy speech by Jesus, which is directly prompted by the indignation of the other disciples at the sons of Zebedee. They most probably regarded the brothers' approach to Jesus as an unfair attempt to settle in their own favor, through a direct appeal, the controversial question they had been discussing earlier. This, at any rate, is how Jesus seems to understand the reaction of the other disciples, when he now replies to all of them as a group and sets out his fundamental position with regard to the striving for power that lies behind this request. He begins by distancing himself very strictly from every form of oppression. He then indicates the alternative. Since these words of Jesus are the most detailed and comprehensive statement in the Gospel about the question of power, we shall offer a more precise exegesis of this passage (Mark 10:42-45):

> 42You know that among the Gentiles
> those who seem to rule subjugate their peoples,
> and their great men misuse their official powers over them.
> 43But it is not so among you!
> Let whoever among you wants to be a great man,
> be your servant,
> 44and let whoever among you wants to be the first,
> be the slave of all.
> 45For the Son of Man too came,
> not to be served,
> but to serve
> and to give his life as a ransom in favor of many.

On verse 42. The picture of the secular rulers as "those who seem to rule" already expresses a clear distance. We shall return below to the rule and the official power of the state, which Jesus employs here as a contrasting picture without, of course, calling it into question as such (cf. Mark 12:17 par.). In the context of this dialogue, Jesus is making a statement not about the power of the state but about the striving for supremacy that finds a particularly clear expression in the structures of political power. Jesus describes this here by means of two participles, each of which is negatively strengthened by the preposition *kata* (against). These unmask what lies behind the disciples' request, namely, the will to have power, in order to enforce one's own interests at the cost of others.

On verse 43a. "But it is not so among you!" With this caveat, Jesus asserts as a fact the otherness of those who belong to him. This negation is more strongly marked in the Greek than in the translation, since Greek (like Hebrew) has two distinct words for negation, depending on whether one is negating a possibility (the subjective negation, *mê*) or a state of affairs (the objective negation, *ou*). In this verse, the objective negation is employed. It is thus not an exhortation ("it ought not to be so among you!") but a statement of fact: "it is not so among you!" Jesus does not present the difference with regard to power as something *desirable.* He affirms clearly that the one who belongs to him *is* different.

On verses 43b and 44. The next words of Jesus tell us what this otherness consists of: true greatness lies in service, in existing for others and making their needs one's own, free from the compulsion to assert oneself and from the urge to dominate. We must note here that, even when he speaks of the "alternative society of salvation"[13] that is oriented to service, Jesus speaks of one who is "great" and "first"—in other words, it is a question of various high positions and thus likewise of power. Jesus does not preach the ideal of a fellowship in which there is no rule. Rather, he recognizes the necessity of superior and lower positions, of command and obedience. But he offers an inverse justification of hierarchy. Among those who follow him, those at the top are not the ones who compel the others to obey them but those who act in the interest of the others and thus realize something of God's caring rule.[14]

On verse 45. Even the ideal of serving can be abused in a terrible way, for rulers are strongly inclined to legitimate themselves as "servants of the state," in order to act in the "correctly understood" interest of the others—and, in cases of doubt, even against the will of the others. It is not by chance that the worst crimes in history were perpetrated by people who alleged, or were even personally convinced, that they were acting as servants of a higher goal. Even the Christian churches were and are not immune to the temptation to abuse power, and the mask of serving made the churches all the more unassailable. The decisive point is that Jesus makes himself the criterion of correct serving not as the master and authoritative teacher but precisely as the one who lays down his life for others. By doing so, he makes it clear that he does not desire, still less exact, sacrifices from others. Rather, he sacrifices himself for others. His authority consists precisely in the fact that he is wholly the "man for others,"[15] who has ransomed the "many" through the ultimate service, namely, the gift of himself, which gives them access to freedom.[16] Jesus then demands that this service should be the form of life of those who follow him. For Jesus, the only "great" or "first" person is one who knows that he or she is completely subordinate to the "thou" of the other. Indeed, we can say more than this: the power that is based on force corrupts its possessors in the long term, but the willingness to serve qualifies a person for leadership. This is why service is "enjoined" upon the disciples "as the conduct of a leader."[17]

When we are told in Mark 10:45 that the Son of Man "has come," this affirmation about his mission points to God's commission as the ultimate reason for Jesus' service and hence also for the alternative dealings with power that have their foundations in God's will and his very being. This means that the title "Son of Man" is appropriate here. Already in the book of Daniel, he is the representative of God's humane and human rule (Dan 7:13-14) in contrast to the world empires that are embodied in the beasts; it is possible that in Mark the context of Vespasian's rule, which was based on military power, also lends this contrast an additional contemporary relevance.[18]

In the Lord's Supper, the total gift of self is explicitly linked to God, when Jesus shares out his body and his blood for the others and interprets this as the establishing of the covenant with God (Mark 14:22-24 par.). This founds a new fellowship that is oriented to the kingdom of God and is perfected in that kingdom (Mark 14:25 par.). Accordingly, the members of this fellowship of salvation that is established through Jesus' gift of self are told that they too must give their lives for others.

The interpretation of Jesus' life as a service is taken up and intensified by the other Gospels, each in its own specific way. Luke underlines even more strongly in his Gospel the significance of the dialogue that we have expounded above, not only by linking it to the disciples' quarrel about which of them is the greatest (so that it concerns all the disciples from the very beginning) but also by consciously moving it to a later position in the narrative, after the Lord's Supper, and making it the prelude to Jesus' farewell discourse. This gives the dialogue an even greater importance, as Jesus' bequest. At the same time, the evangelist has reformulated Jesus' answer in such a way that he speaks of himself directly in the first person. By means of the diatribic structure of question and answer, he first emphasizes the contempt in which serving was held in the general consciousness. Then, through an adversative "I am" logion, he highlights, as the special character of the life of Jesus, the unheard-of fact that the Lord here becomes the servant of his servants:

> For who is greater,
> the one who sits at the table or the one who serves [him]?
> Is it not the one at the table?
> But I am among you as one who serves. (Luke 22:27)

This is now the second time in the Gospel of Luke that Jesus, as the Lord, turns the system of rule upside down through his service. We find a similarly bold affirmation in the first eschatological unit that is inserted into the travel narrative. Jesus exhorts the disciples to be ready always for service (Luke 12:35), and he justifies this admonition by means of a parable that evokes the scene of a banquet (as in Luke 22:27) and pronounces a beatitude on those servants whom the Lord finds awake on his return. He promises them:

> Blessed are those slaves
> whom the master finds alert when he comes;
> amen, I tell you,
> he will fasten his belt and have them sit down to eat,
> and he will come and serve them. (Luke 12:37)

In Luke, mutual service "is made" more strongly "transparent to the future services of leadership in the community"[19] than in the Gospel of Mark, and it is even more explicitly based on the relationship to God. The evangelist makes this clear in a programmatic manner already at the beginning of his Gospel. The Lukan prehistory emphasizes the greatness of God by means of divine predicates such as "Lord," "Mighty," and "Most High." At the same time, Luke shows that the greatness of this God, who reveals himself in the lowliness of a child, consists in the fact that, instead of making others small, he raises them up and gives them a great name.[20] The prehistory is consciously formed by the evangelist as a preliminary sign that indicates how the life and the message of Jesus in the Gospel are to be read. The end of the Gospel corresponds to this: the Son of God, who has lived his life as service up to his death, is exalted by God to his right hand. The Gospel of Luke depicts this in a highly dramatic form in the ascension, which only it relates.

This link between service and exaltation is also the criterion for the behavior of Jesus' followers. The Lukan Jesus explicitly exhorts his disciples twice, in the form of a summary (Luke 14:11; 18:4-5),[21] not to exalt themselves over the others but to humble themselves, because in this way they will be exalted[22] by the God "in whose sight the arrogance of human beings is an abomination" (Luke 16:15) and who has chosen "to give the kingdom" to the "little flock" (Luke 12:32). The human conduct that corresponds to this is made concrete in Luke not least in a "serving" use of one's property.[23]

In the Gospel of Matthew, Jesus explains his call in the "Savior's tender invitation" to those "that are weary and are carrying heavy burdens" by saying that his yoke is easy and his burden light, because he himself is "gentle and humble in heart" (Matt 11:29). This self-description is underlined once again, as an interpretation of the alternative rule of the Messiah, by means of the reflective quotation that the evangelist forms from Isaiah 62:11 and Zechariah 9:9 when Jesus enters Jerusalem:

> Tell the daughter of Zion,
> Look, your king is coming to you,
> humble, and mounted on a donkey,
> and on a colt, the foal of a donkey. (Matt 21:5)

In the third beatitude in the Sermon on the Mount, Jesus promises that the one who follows this lowly king and is himself "gentle" will be given lordship over the earth (Matt 5:5). In his community discourse, the Matthean Jesus answers the disciples' question about who is greater in the kingdom of heaven by putting a child in their midst and demanding a radical reorientation:

> Amen, I tell you,
> unless you change and become like children,
> you will never enter the kingdom of heaven.
> Whoever becomes humble like this child
>   is the greatest in the kingdom of heaven.

Whoever welcomes one such child in my name
welcomes me. (18:3-5)

This demand that one should make oneself lowly like a child goes beyond the Markan source. Jesus thus establishes at the very start of his discourse "an ethos of humility and lowliness as the ethical guideline,"[24] and he links this ethos directly to his own person, since the last sentence makes it clear "that no one less than Jesus himself is encountered in the child."[25] He then lays down this "ethical guideline" in his discourse against the Pharisees as the distinguishing mark of discipleship, in contrast to the self-display of the Pharisees. In the community of Jesus' followers (as he has already demanded at Matt 20:24-28), the members are not to outdo one another but to serve one another as brothers and sisters, that is to say, as members of the *familia Dei*, since this is what sets them apart:

But you are not to be called Rabbi,
for you have one teacher,
and you are all brothers and sisters.
And call no one on earth your father,
for you have one Father—the one in heaven.
Nor are you to be called instructors,
for you have one instructor, the Christ.
The greatest among you
will be your servant.
But whoever exalts himself
will be made low,
and whoever makes himself low
will be exalted. (Matt 23:8-12)

At the end of the final discourse of Jesus, in the narrative of the last judgment that closes his eschatological discourse, the actions of love that he demands are called "serving" (Matt 25:42-44). The immediate addressees of this serving are those in need, but the indirect addressee is Christ, the Son of Man who is exalted to become king and judge, and who identifies unreservedly with those who are "least," when he says:

> Amen, I tell you,
> whatever you did to the least of these members of my family,
> you did it to me. (25:40; cf. 25:46)

Finally, the fourth Gospel paints what is perhaps the most powerful picture of the serving Jesus. At the Last Supper (cf. Luke 22:27), Jesus, acting explicitly as the "teacher" and "Lord" of his "servants" (John 13:12-17), binds a slave's apron around his waist and washes the feet of his disciples (13:1-11). It is precisely in the Gospel that most strongly emphasizes the sovereignty of the Son, and can indeed call him "God" three times (1:1, 18; 20:28), that the scene of the washing of the disciples' feet shows plainly that the Son of God is the Lord as the one who serves.

It is not by chance that the washing of the feet comes at the beginning of the farewell discourses, since it points to Jesus' laying down of his life.[26] If one reads this against the background of striking logia such as "whoever has seen me has seen the Father" (John 14:9) or "I and the Father are one" (10:30), it becomes clear that, in John, Jesus' service is an integral part of the mission he has received from the Father.[27] At the same time, the fourth Gospel emphasizes that Jesus' conduct is the norm for the disciples' dealings with one another. Jesus comments as follows on the washing of the feet:

> For I have set you an example,
> that you also should do
> as I have done to you. (John 13:15)

In the farewell discourses, Jesus' laying down of his life is interpreted as the way in which the divine love is given shape. The disciples' behavior toward one another is to be in accordance with this love (15:12-15). John too emphasizes here that service does not abase but rather exalts: they are no longer slaves but become the friends of Jesus (15:14-15) and in the end even his brothers and sisters (20:17). The Johannine Christ can also say that the Father honors the one who serves him (12:26); these words recall the logion that is transmitted once by Matthew and twice by Luke, that the one who lowers himself will be exalted.

Irrespective of how much of the individual logia and scenes go back to the historical Jesus and how much was later attributed to him, these texts in all the four Gospels, taken as a whole, attest that Jesus Christ, who was venerated as Lord, was remembered as one who lived as a man for others and who had authority precisely as the one who served.[28] The picture of this serving Lord then left its imprint on the Christian ethos in the Letters of Paul and in the writings of both his immediate and his indirect pupils.

The Service of the Believers in the Epistolary Literature

When Luther in his treatise *On the Freedom of a Christian* speaks of the "two contradictory statements" to the effect that the Christian is "a free lord over all things and subject to no one" and at the same time "a ministering servant of all things and subject to everyone,"[29] he is describing the interpenetration of faith and love that Paul elaborates especially in the Letter to the Galatians. The fellowship with God as Father, which is established in faith, makes slaves—that is to say, fallen creatures—free children of God (Gal 4:3-7; Rom 8:14-16). At the same time, the consequence of being determined by the Spirit (cf. Gal 4:6; Rom 8:14) is a new bond to one's neighbors, since faith becomes active in love (Gal 5:6). Accordingly, freedom is "not 'restricted' by *love*, but is incarnated in love and appears in the form of *servitude*":[30]

> For you were called to freedom, brothers and sisters;
> only do not use your freedom as an opportunity for the flesh,
> but through love become slaves to one another.
> For the whole law is summed up in a single commandment,
> "You shall love your neighbor as yourself." (Gal 5:13-14)

When Paul understands the love of neighbor that takes the concrete form of service as the summary of the Torah, this makes it clear—as does the logion of Jesus at Mark 12:29-30 par.—that love of God and love of neighbor are directly connected. In Matthew 25:44, the service of one's neighbor is in reality the service of Christ, and Paul too sees these as inseparable.[31] The apostle represents the basic image of the serving Jesus to imprint this like an embossed stamp (*tupos*) on the community.[32] The paraenesis in Romans 12:9-21 is particularly instructive. Here, the apostle mentions in the same breath the service of Christ (Rom 12:11) and the love for one's fellow human being. And this love must be shown not only to the members of the community (Rom 12:9-10; 13.15-16) but even to the hostile fellow human beings outside the community (Rom 12:14, 17-21). This is why, already in the earliest community, the "service of the word" is accompanied by the "daily service" of the needy. The church, as Acts 6:1-7 describes it, is always also *diakonia*.

The First Letter of Peter likewise underlines the link between worship and service. The author justifies the freedom of the Christians by speaking of their service of God (1 Pet 2:16). In the first summary of its paraenesis, at 1 Peter 4:7-11,[33] the Letter demands that the believers, as "good stewards of the manifold grace of God," should "serve one another" with the gifts of grace they have received (1 Pet 4:10). Just as the service has its origin in God's care for his people and flows from the gifts of grace and the strength that he bestows, so too the reciprocal service that unites the community in love (cf. 1 Pet 4:8-9) should lead in turn to the praise of God:

Whoever serves
must do so with the strength that God supplies,
so that God may be glorified in all things through Jesus
Christ.
To him belong the glory and the power forever and ever.
Amen. (1 Pet 4:11)

The Church Ministries as Services

While reciprocal service is the task shared by all Christians, the various writings in the New Testament apply the category of service in a special way to the positions of leadership within the community. Every church ministry can be called a service (Rom 12:7; 1 Pet 4:10; Acts 6:1; 1 Cor 12:5; 16:15), and this term is used most directly in the case of the deacons (Phil 1:1; 1 Tim 3:8-13). Similarly, all office bearers can be called slaves or servants of God (2 Cor 11:23; 1 Pet 2:16; Rev 7:3; 19:2; cf. Acts 16:17) or of Christ (1 Cor 7:22; cf. John 12:26). We hear of the "service of the word" (Acts 6:4) or of the "servants of the new covenant" (2 Cor 3:6). In this sense, Paul also consistently calls his apostleship a service (Rom 11:13; 2 Cor 4:1; 5:18; 6:3; et passim).[34] This is especially clear at the start of the Letters, where not only the apostle[35] but also the pupils who write in his name[36] and other Letter writers[37] pointedly call themselves slaves of Christ (Jesus) or of the Lord, a "slave of God and of the Lord Jesus Christ" (Jas 1:1), or a "slave of God" (Titus 1:1).[38] Paul certainly expresses his own special position by using this language. But since he justifies his authority through the attachment to Christ, every form of hierarchy in the nascent church is oriented and subordinated to this one Lord, and every arbitrary use of the precedence that is linked to such a hierarchy is implicitly rejected.

Both the epistolary literature and the Jesus tradition that is transmitted in the Gospels agree on the central importance of the category of service for the way Christians deal with each other, especially for the positions of leadership. The simplest explanation of this fact is that the apostle and his pupils, as well as the other Letter writers, have recourse to precisely this tradition. In his paraenesis, Paul repeatedly refers explicitly to Jesus' exemplary service (cf. Rom 15:7ff.); he can also justify the demands he makes by appealing to the self-abasement of the Son of God when he took on "the form of a slave" (Phil 2:7)—a self-abasement that ultimately led to his death.[39]

The State as the Servant of God

What we have said up to this point might give the impression that service in the presence of God and for one's neighbor applies only to the sphere of the believers and that nothing but violence and oppression rules outside this sphere. This impression is no accident, since logia such as John 15:18-21 posit a clear-cut contrast between the group of disciples and their conduct, which is determined by love, on the one hand, and the hatred of the world, on the other hand; and Mark 10:42-45 highlights the service of the Christian fellowship against the contrasting background of lordship in the world, which is identified with oppression and the abuse of power. But this black-and-white picture is not all that the New Testament has to say about the state and its power. For since God is the Lord of all the world, he is able, through the power of the state, to impose order, to enforce his will even in a reality in which conflict and violence are facts that cannot always be eliminated. The state's power protects the sphere of everyday life, even by the use of counterforce where necessary. When power is ensured by the threat of violence, the risk of abuse is ever present, and this is reflected in the texts mentioned above; but state governance is not bad per se. On the contrary, the New Testament can see a positive relationship between it and the will of God.

This is already hinted at in the synoptic tradition, when Jesus is asked about paying taxes in Mark 12:13-17 par. He demands not only that one give God what belongs to God but also that one give the state what is its due. Paul goes even further. He requires his readers to pay the taxes they owe (Rom 13:7), but he also applies to state power the category of service, which Jesus had applied to his followers as the antithesis of the abuse of power by "those who seem to rule." Paul does so in the double sense, namely, that the service of human beings is the service of God and that the service of God is the service of human beings. He formulates his celebrated statements about the state in the thirteenth chapter of the Letter to the Romans. They stand out because of their self-contained and fundamental character:

> [1]Let every person be subject to the governing authorities;
> for there is no authority except from God,
> and those authorities that exist have been instituted by God.
> [2]Therefore:
> whoever resists authority
> resists what God has appointed,
> and those who resist will incur judgment.
> [3]For rulers are not a terror to good conduct,
> but to bad.
> Do you wish to have no fear of the authority?
> Then do what is good, and you will receive its approval;
> [4]for it is God's servant for your good.
> But if you do what is wrong, you should be afraid,
> for the authority does not bear the sword in vain!
> It is the servant of God to execute wrath on the wrongdoer.
> [5]Therefore one must be subject,
> not only because of wrath
> but also because of conscience.
> [6]For the same reason you also pay taxes,
> for the authorities are God's servants, busy with this very
> thing [i.e., this service].

> [7]Pay to all what is due them—
> taxes to whom taxes are due,
> revenue to whom revenue is due,
> respect to whom respect is due,
> honor to whom honor is due. (Rom 13:1-7)

These words, which for a long time were regarded in Protestantism as the essential basis for the definition of the relationship between Christians and the state, appear at first sight to be a religious "blank check" for state authority, which it legitimates unconditionally as deriving its rule directly from God, no matter how that rule may in fact have been attained. In this context, every resistance to the authorities takes on the appearance of resistance to God. One example of the problems connected with such an interpretation is the Ansbach Memorandum,[40] which was drawn up in 1934 by a theological working party in the National Socialist Union of Protestant Pastors. Its members included W. Ehlert and P. Althaus, both of whom were professors in Erlangen, and it was a direct reaction to the Theological Declaration of Barmen, which had been drawn up by the Confessing Church. The memorandum affirms that God reveals himself not only in Christ but equally in family, people, and race. Accordingly, the signatories understood the National Socialist state, and its führer, Adolf Hitler, as a God-given ordering of society that likewise possesses the character of divine revelation.[41] The presupposition of such a claim is found inter alia in the fourth thesis: "as Christians, we honor, with gratitude to God, every ordering of society, and thus every authority, even in disfigurement."[42]

It must be said that the highly apodictic formulations of the apostle, especially in Romans 13:1, do not exclude a priori the possibility of such an interpretation. We do not know why Paul expresses himself so unguardedly here, although he was very well aware of the blindness of rulers (cf. 1 Cor 2:8). Perhaps one factor is that in the early period of Nero's reign, when the Letter to the Romans was written, he did not envisage the problem of a fundamentally perverted use of power by the state (to say nothing of the monstrosities of the National Socialist rule). Although the apostle himself certainly did not experience only good treatment at the hands of the state (cf. 2 Cor 11:25), the Acts of the Apostles show that the legal order that was defended by the authorities occasionally saved him from being lynched by the mob (Acts 16:35-40; 18:12-16; 19:35-40) and made possible his "appeal to Caesar" (Acts 25:9-12). It is no longer possible to determine whether other circumstances at that time[43] caused Paul to bring the state into such close proximity to God that every resistance to the state immediately takes on the appearance of disobedience to God.

At any rate, in the aftermath of the cruel persecution of the Christians at the end of Nero's reign, we find a greater differentiation in the assessment of the role of the state in the New Testament and early Christian writings. It is indeed true that, as late as in the Gospel of John, Jesus as defendant can tell Pilate that the governor's power has been given to him "from above," that is to say, from God (John 19:11); but the continuation—"Therefore the one who handed me over to you is guilty of a greater sin"—already shows that, even if the authority of the state comes from above, not everything that the state does is sanctioned from above. And when the First Letter of Peter transmits the affirmations of Romans 13:17, it is clear that it has greater reservations about the direct link between God's will and the power of the state. The author no longer calls the state the servant of God: it is only a human institution (1 Pet 2:13), which no longer deserves *phobos* (respect), as is probably the case in Romans 13:7, but only *timê* (honor).[44]

We find differentiations in the Lukan double work too. In the Acts of the Apostles, Peter emphatically declares to the Sanhedrin, the "high council," that one must obey God rather than human beings (Acts 5:29; cf. 4:19). The statement by the devil in the Lukan version of the temptation narrative is indirect but relatively drastic: he justifies his offer to Jesus of the kingdoms of the earth by saying that all these kingdoms have been handed over to him (Luke 4:6). It is possible to see the verb *paradedotai* (have been handed over) in Luke 4:6 as a *passivum divinum*, so that a divine ordinance lies behind the handing over of power to Satan. Nevertheless, the allocation of rule in the world to the sphere that is subject to the devil presupposes no little tension between such rule and the will of God.

The Revelation of John goes even further. Here, the servant of God has become nothing other than the handmaid of evil. In view of the increasing tensions, which (probably in the last years of Emperor Domitian) could even lead to martyrdoms (cf. Rev 6:9-10; 17:6; 18:24), the seer sees the Roman rule only as the "harlot Babylon," drunk with the blood of the saints (Rev 17:1ff.), as a murderous agent of the power that is opposed to God.

Although such a demonization of the power of the state remains the exception in Christianity, it leaves no doubt, when taken in conjunction with the other passages we have quoted, that one cannot appeal exclusively to Romans 13:1-7 to ascribe divine legitimacy in the name of the New Testament to every rule "even in disfigurement." However, Paul's words have a perennial importance because they played a central role in preventing early Christianity from simply rejecting state order and its institutions, even at a time when the Christians were societally marginalized and under pressure. Instead, the early Christians were able to see a positive relationship between the state and the divine will and thus to take their place in the structures of society, to the extent that this was compatible with their faith. This is why the later tradition normally regarded obedience and submission to the power of the state and intercession for the authorities as an obligation for Christians (cf. Titus 3:1; 1 Tim 2:1-2; *1 Clem.* 61.1-2).

If we are to understand the exact meaning of the position Paul takes in Romans 13:1-7, this text must be read in the context of the Letter to the Romans.[45] We notice at once that the apostle has positioned his fundamental declaration about the power of the state in the midst of his remarks about love, where it seems out of place. He has previously demanded love within the community and the renunciation of vengeance on outsiders. This culminates in the requirement not to repay evil with evil but to "overcome evil with good" (Rom 12:9-21). Immediately after the passage about the authorities, Paul says that love is "the fulfilling of the law" (Rom 13:8-10). It can scarcely be by chance that the apostle interrupts the connectedness of his remarks about love with this passage about the state authorities. Rather, he wishes thereby to make it clear that God does not leave the good unprotected in a world that is far from being determined only by love. God has established the state as a good ordering (*taxis*), in order to preserve—if need be, by the sword—a space for life and hence also to protect the Christians.[46] Like the love that Romans 12:9 demands, the power of the state is active on behalf of the good and against evil; and as the avenger of evil (Rom 13:4), it does what God does (according to Rom 12:19) when he is confronted with the injustice that is inflicted on the Christians. Since the power of the state acts in accordance with the divine will and action, by thus ensuring a sphere that protects the good, it is to be respected by Christians as the servant of God, and they are to support it by paying their taxes.

This accolade applies not least to the armed servants of the state.[47] The state and its representatives are not only *diakonoi poleôs* (servants of civil society)[48] but also servants of God. This accolade is thus also an obligation, and this means that we must reverse the link in the justification: the power of the state is the servant of God only when it does not bend the law but uses its monopoly on force to safeguard life in civil society—for in that way, it serves human beings in accordance with God's loving will. P. Althaus, one of the authors of the above-mentioned Ansbach Memorandum, rightly noted in his commentary on Romans as early as 1938 that the "authorities" in the sense of Romans 13 are not sufficiently defined by the mere possession of power. More is needed, namely, "that the administration of power be at the service of *an ethically determined legal order.*"[49]

But even with this clarification, such a service on the part of the state power belongs to the "form of this world" that is passing away (1 Cor 7:31). The service concerns the responsible use of the state power, including the inherently destructive force of the "sword," which was wielded in the New Testament period exclusively by pagans.[50] This means, first of all, that the state enforces the will of God, since it ensures the preservation of a legal order through the force that is subject to the law, in a world in which the kingdom of God is not yet realized and violence is a force that cannot yet be eliminated. Second, a distinction must be drawn between the sovereignty of the state and the sovereignty of God that is introduced by Christ (cf. 1 Cor 15:23-28), in which God will be all in all. The Pax Augusta of the Imperium Romanum is not the *shalôm* of the kingdom of God that is defined by the Holy Spirit (Rom 14:17). In the state, God's will is realized in the form of a countervailing force that is devoid of grace.[51] This means that his will is realized only indirectly.

The dignity of the state is the charge it has received from God, the task of keeping evil at bay. But this task is also its boundary. It is not only where it tramples the law under foot that the state ceases to be the servant of God. Where it goes beyond its charge to be "God's governance on the left hand" (as Luther puts it) and wants itself to bring about the perfecting of the world—in other words, where it puts itself in the place of God—it can no longer appeal to divine legitimation. This is because—as the history of the modern age has repeatedly shown in a drastic manner—when the attempt is made to establish through violence the ideal state that is one's aim, the absolutized virtue turns into terror.[52]

The kingdom of God can be established only by God himself. But it is already penetrating this world wherever the conduct of believers is in accordance with what all four Gospels understand as the very core of the life of Jesus: the pro-existence that manifests itself in loving devotion and the gift of self.[53] This sphere is determined not by an external ordering but by love. Unlike the service in the kingdom "on the left hand," love trusts in the power of God alone and can therefore itself renounce violence (cf. Rom 12:19-21; Luke 6:27-36 par. Matt 5:38-48) in order to overcome evil with good (Rom 12:19-21). Love's only weapons are the "weapons of light" (Rom 13:12), even when this still entails suffering. This is why the two framing beatitudes at the beginning of the Sermon on the Mount emphasize that the "kingdom of heaven" is promised to the "poor in spirit," who are still being "persecuted for righteousness' sake" (Matt 5:3, 10).

The coming of the kingdom of God to the earth cannot be a program of human action; it can be obtained only by prayer. This, however, does not mean that one must hold self-righteously aloof from "dirty" politics. Rather, the fact that the believers are not responsible for the ultimate things means that they are responsible before God for the penultimate things.[54] This also includes the willingness to assume responsibility in the political and societal sphere so that God's will can be enforced there too. In this sense, Jeremiah had in the past asked the exiles in Babylon—the state that had conquered their land, destroyed the temple, and carried them off into exile—to "seek the welfare of the city" and to "pray to the Lord on its behalf" (Jer 29:7). Accordingly, the First Letter to Timothy not only exhorts the believers to pray for all persons but demands a special intercession "for the emperors and all who are in high positions" (1 Tim 2:1-3; cf. also *1 Clem.* 61.1), although the relationship was certainly not free of tensions, as the Revelation of John, which was written about the same time, shows. The circumstances were unfavorable, to put it mildly; but, even at that period, it was expected that where possible the believers would pray to God for those who held political responsibility and for their work.

Paul sums up the attitude that lies behind such a service—a trustful renunciation of the arbitrary use of power, willingness to suffer, the "poverty in spirit" (Matt 5:3) that is accompanied in the Sermon on the Mount inter alia by gentleness (Matt 5:5), mercy (Matt 5:7), and working for peace (Matt 5:9)—as *tapeinophrosunê* (humility).

Chapter 3

Humility

The Biblical Evidence

The noun *tapeinophrosunê*, usually translated as "humility," is attested in the literature of classical antiquity for the first time in the New Testament: in Paul, at Philippians 2:3. It is unlikely that the apostle himself coined this word, since it is used at a slightly later date and without any recognizable dependence on Paul, both by the Jewish historian Josephus[1] and by the Stoic philosopher Epictetus.[2] In these passages, however, as with the semantic field *tapeinos ktl.* (lowly or humble) outside the literature that is influenced by the New Testament, it has a negative meaning that lies, depending on the context, somewhere between sycophancy and pusillanimity, servility and shabbiness. Paul, however, established a direct relationship between this word and the Christ event, thereby making it an ideal of Christian ethics,[3] as we can see in his sphere of influence, from the Letter to the Ephesians via the First Letter of Peter to the Lukan double work, and then further (see below).[4]

This revolutionary transformation of a negative term into an ideal is rooted in Paul's theology of the cross, but it is not without support in the tradition that was transmitted to him. A somewhat narrower Old Testament tradition and a broader early Jewish tradition,[5] in addition to some logia of Jesus,[6] attest a high religious appreciation of lowliness, which Paul takes up, as we have already seen, with regard to "service."

God's election is understood already in the Old Testament as an action taken on behalf of the lowly:

> Let Israel be glad in its Maker;
> let the children of Zion rejoice in their King . . .
> For the Lord takes pleasure in his people;
> he adorns the humble with victory. (Ps 149:2, 4)

Conversely, God resists the opposite attitude of pride and arrogance. We have already seen this in the song of Hannah and the Magnificat of Mary,[7] but it is found in other passages too:

> The Lord overthrows the thrones of the proud,
> and enthrones the lowly in their place.
> The Lord plucks up the roots of the nations,
> and plants the humble in their place. (Sir 10:14-15)[8]

The Letter of Aristeas formulates it as follows: "God, in accordance with his nature, receives that which humbles itself" (Arist. 257). This link between lowliness and closeness to God also explains why the early Jewish sapiential literature can say that, just as arrogance leads to a fall (Prov 16:18) and to disgrace (Prov 11:2), so humility leads to honor (Prov 15:33; 18:12; 29:23) and consequently wisdom is with the humble (Prov 11:2). As an expression of the only attitude that is appropriate before God, humility therefore constitutes the path to a successful life:

> The reward for humility and fear of the Lord
> is riches and honor and life. (Prov 22:4)

As we have seen, lowliness and gentleness were an essential component of Jesus' self-understanding. We have seen this in his words about serving, and it is confirmed by other logia too (cf. Mark 10:15). Indeed, A. Schlatter could begin a study of Jesus with the following thesis: "one who seriously tackles the question of Jesus' own relationship to faith is confronted with the humility of Jesus."[9] There is only one formulation in the Gospel tradition in which Jesus calls himself *tapeinos tê[i] kardia[i]*, which we can translate as "humble" (Matt 11:29). It was Paul who employed the noun *tapeinophrosunê* as a concept that expressed the positive appreciation of the attitude that refrains from self-exaltation.[10]

It is first in the sphere of influence of the Pauline theology that humility is given a home. After the Letters to the Colossians and the Ephesians, the First Letter of Peter represents the next important stage on the path taken by the ideal of humility, because here, for the first time, humility becomes a central concept of ethics. It is no longer—as in the Letters to the Philippians, the Colossians, and the Ephesians—only one among several modes of conduct that are determined by love and consideration of others. Now humility becomes the foundation of one's relationship both to one's fellow human beings and to God. Outside the immediate sphere of Pauline influence, humility plays a role for the first time in the Letter of James, in the context of its critique of wealth and greed and of the lack of internal and external peace that is their fruit.[11] Through these paraenetic passages in the epistles, humility acquires its established place in church history, beginning with the *First Letter of Clement*.[12] Origen sees it as faith's alternative to the arrogance of sin; for him it is the "virtue in absolute terms, which encompasses all the other virtues."[13] The Rule of Benedict devotes its seventh and most detailed chapter to humility and interprets it as a ladder leading up to heaven on twelve rungs that ascend from *timor Dei*, the fear of God as judge, up to *caritas*, the love in which there is no more fear.

The Suspect Virtue

Despite this, the word "humility" occurs rather seldom today not only in the general vocabulary but also in that of the church. The reasons for this lie not least in the "ruinous history"[14] of the abuse that has been perpetrated with the aid of the ideal of humility. Broadly speaking, there are three basic types of this abuse.

First, this term has been used in order to tell others, in the name of Christianity, that they must be subordinate—in other words, in order to exercise power over them. Humility was recommended above all to women, to obligate them to a selfless service. But a humility that was prescribed in this manner became a humiliation.[15]

Second, an additional factor was often the hypocrisy of which Kierkegaard wrote: "Christianity . . . taught humility, but not everyone learned humility. . . . Hypocrisy learned how to change its mask, and remained the same, or . . . became even worse."[16] This covers up a claim to power that Friedrich Nietzsche exposed in his mocking correction to the logion of Jesus at Luke 18:14: "the one who humbles himself wants to be raised up."[17]

Third, while the first two types involve the religious concealment of the will for power, a third risk in the idea of humility is the obsessiveness of pathological self-denial. Where humility is no longer a self-limitation in favor of the other but takes the form of a self-diminution that is per se a religious virtue, it becomes destructive. Let us hear Nietzsche once again: "the Gospel of the 'lowly ones' makes people lowly."[18]

When we speak of humility, we must always bear in mind these possibilities that the idea of humility may be distorted and abused; these possibilities are probably as old as the concept itself.[19] Here too, however, the scholastic principle *abusus non tollit usum* applies. In other words, the possibility of abusing something must not be applied a priori to discredit the thing itself. In what follows, we shall see that although the New Testament statements about humility are open to being misunderstood in the sense set out above—especially where these statements are detached from the context of the biblical argumentation and self-diminution is proclaimed as a virtue—in its original meaning, humility has absolutely nothing in common with humiliation, hypocrisy, and obsessiveness.[20]

This perception seems to be gaining renewed influence today. It is striking to see that this suspect word is suddenly being employed more frequently in public discourse and with a decidedly positive meaning. This may also be a reaction to the financial crisis that was caused by ruthless investment banking and to the shocks this crisis inflicted on a way of thinking that was fixated exclusively on maximizing profits.

However, the controversial character of humility is not due only to the history of its abuse. Another factor is that, like service, humility too demands of the human being something that accords only to a very limited degree with his nature, which is programmed to promote self-assertion. Let us begin, therefore, by indicating the place occupied by humility in the overall context of Pauline theology.

The Ethos of the Cross

Criticism of the idea of humility is not a specific characteristic of the modern period. "Humility" was an inflammatory term already in classical antiquity, a culture that was oriented to the ideal of the free man and of his honor.[21] For example, the Stoic philosopher Epictetus criticizes it as an undignified self-abasement.[22] It is indeed true that the word group *tapeinos ktl.* can sometimes also denote something positive in classical literature, in that the human being in question is not behaving presumptuously.[23] This means that A. Dihle's verdict that the idea of humility is foreign "to the whole of ancient ethics"[24] is perhaps somewhat too apodictic;[25] and we may add, with H. Wojtkowiak, that even the pagan "ethos [offers] a point of contact for the demand for an attitude of lowliness, that is to say, the good of the community."[26] In general, however, it remains true that nothing outside the Jewish-Christian sphere corresponds to the ideal formulated by Paul, that one should regard the other in humility as higher than one's own self (Phil 2:3),[27] not least because this ideal is in direct tension with the "agonistic ideal of life,"[28] the urge to find one's own honor in outdoing the others. According to H. I. Marrou, this is summarized in words of Homer that were quoted again and again as a leitmotif of education in the classical period: "always to be the best and superior to the others."[29] This aphorism sounds like the conscious antithesis of the ideal of humility, and this tension makes the acrimony in the ancient critique of the idea of humility more readily comprehensible. For despite all the polemic, more is involved than an intentional distortion when the enemies of Christianity equate humility with servile submissiveness and vehemently reject it.[30] Their reaction reveals an incompatibility with their value system, and this becomes clear when we bear in mind that the Christian (re)interpretation of *tapeinophrosunê*, which we could paraphrase freely as an "orientation of existence and of conduct that restrains oneself to the benefit of the other person," is one of a number of positive "rebrandings" of designations of social status that had negative connotations; one prominent example is the "serving" (*diakonein, douleuein*) that was discussed in the previous chapter.[31] Christianity thus gave pointed expression to its "transvaluation of values" (which was oriented to the revelation of God in Jesus' life and in his gift of self), in terms of its relationship to power, status, and honor—and this was bound to provoke the agonistic ideal of life, which was oriented to the acquisition of status. The high esteem for serving, which probably goes back to the historical Jesus, belongs in this context. Paul has defined it more precisely by means of the category of humility, in view of the attitude that lies behind serving.

Humility as Existence "in Christ": Philippians 2 and Romans 12

The earliest passage in Greek literature in which the concept of *tapeinophrosunê* is attested belongs to the paraenetic section in Philippians 2:1-11, which consists of two parts. Verses 1-4, which are one single connected sentence, contain the paraenesis properly speaking, that is to say, the exhortation and encouragement, while verses 6-11 quote a hymn about Christ in justification of the paraenesis. The two parts are joined together by verse 5, which forms the hinge. Since the style of the hymn, with its rhythmic structure and its partly un-Pauline terminology, is clearly distinct from the context, it is frequently regarded as a pre-Pauline hymn about Christ that Paul has integrated into the Letter.[32] Other scholars assume Pauline authorship and point out that, despite all its distinctive features, the hymn is relatively closely interwoven with the context.[33] Another explanation of the relative independence vis-à-vis the context could be that the apostle inserts a hymn that he himself has composed at an earlier date. But whatever the answer to these questions may be, the important point here is that, just as service is traced back in Mark 10:45 to Jesus and the laying down of his life, so too Paul establishes a direct relationship between the humility that he demands and the story of Christ. In justification of his demand, he has appended the hymnic passage that interprets the incarnation as the path of self-abasement even to death. God's response to this self-abasement is the exaltation of Jesus.

Let us look briefly at the context of this passage. We could call the community in Philippi the favorite community of the apostle,[34] and this Letter is the most personal missive of the apostle, the one that of all his Letters best fits the classical genre of the letter of friendship. This also leaves its mark on the argumentation of the Letter. The preceding verses (Phil 1:27-30) are concerned with the preservation of the community against external opponents.[35] The topic in 2:1-11 is the preservation of internal unity:

> 1If then there is any encouragement[36] in Christ,
> if any consolation from love,
> if any sharing in the Spirit,
> if any compassion and sympathy,
> 2make my joy complete:
> be of the same mind,
> having the same love,
> being intent upon being one, as one heart and one soul.
> 3Do nothing from selfish ambition or conceit [literally: the striving for empty honor],
> but in humility let each regard the other as better than himself.
> 4Let each of you look not to his own interests,
> but also[37] to the interests of others.
> 5Let the same mind be in you
> that also [corresponds to your being] in Christ.
> 6He, who was in a divine mode of being,
> did not regard being equal with God
> as an easily-taken prey,[38]
> 7but emptied himself,
> taking the mode of being of a slave,
> and became equal with human beings.
> And being found in human form,
> 8he humbled himself [and]
> became obedient to the point of death—
> even death on a cross.

9Therefore God also highly exalted him
and gave him the name
that is above every name,
10so that at the name of Jesus
every knee should bend,
of things in heaven and on earth and under the earth,
11and every tongue should confess:
The Lord [is] Jesus Christ,
to prove the glory of God [as] the Father.

On verse 1. By beginning with the fourfold "if," Paul mentions and indeed conjures up the very foundations that have already been laid for ethics in the community through the acceptance of the Gospel. This is why the emphasis in the first four half sentences is not on the obligation but on the new being of the members of the community: on the encouragement that comes from faith, on the consolation that comes from love, on the community established by the Spirit, and on the mercy and compassion that result from this. These are all realities that come from God and unite the members of the community in the most direct manner,[39] since their reality is marked by the mercy of God, which has come to determine their lives "in Christ."

On verse 2. This encouragement is followed in verses 2-4 by a demand, namely, the exhortation to unity. The conscious employment of parallelisms here prepares the readers for the hymn. Paul refrains here too from formulating his demand in the imperative. In keeping with the genre of the letter of friendship, he presents it as a request. When he writes, "Make my joy complete," the apostle, not without rhetorical skill, acknowledges the good that is already present in the community, and at the same time he uses his personal bond to the community as a motivation for his exhortations.[40] The demand that is implicit here is now set out in the following passage, down to the end of verse 4. We also find in other Pauline Letters the exhortation to be intent upon one and the same thing.[41] The verb *phronein* (to be of a mind) is a favorite Pauline word, which elsewhere designates the new orientation of thinking and willing that is generated by fellowship with Christ;[42] it is also one component of the noun *tapeinophrosunê*, "humility." It denotes the inner orientation of believers, the "reflecting and aspiring" that underlies and encompasses their thinking, willing, and acting. This disposition, this *phronein*, must repeatedly be fine-tuned in their mutual relations and directed toward the common goal. This is affirmed in verse 2 through two participial elaborations. The first of these mentions love, which Paul had presupposed in verse 1 as the "consolation from [the] love [of God]." He now expects that the members of the community will hold fast to love and transmit it in their dealings with one another. The second elaboration, once more with the verb *phronein*, demands again that they be of one mind. This is further intensified through the adjective *sumpsukhos*, an expression that means something like the "consonance of souls."[43] We have translated it here by means of the hendiadys as "one heart and one soul."[44]

On verses 3-4. In the next two verses, Paul defines through two antitheses the concrete form that unity is to take. Each draws a contrast between the conduct that is presupposed as undesirable and the attitude that is desired. Verse 3 speaks first of "selfish ambition and conceit," a way of behaving where an individual's speaking and striving are aimed at making him great. The apostle frequently uses the verb *phusiousthai* (to puff oneself up, to inflate oneself) in 1 Corinthians to speak of this.[45] This metaphor vividly depicts behavior through which one makes oneself appear bigger, thus driving others to the margins and depriving them of room to breathe.

Humility is contrasted with this puffed-up self-inflation, as the disposition of those who take a step backward and allow others to come forward. Paul expresses this very precisely when he says, "Let each regard the other as better than himself." In Romans 12:10, the "mutual affection" becomes concrete when the Christians "outdo one another in showing honor"; similarly, humility means allowing one's fellow human being to be recognized in his own right, even at the cost of one's own craving for recognition. "The starting point of humility's thinking is the other."[46] This means that, like Jesus, Paul does not demand that the human person should make himself small before an overwhelmingly powerful God but that he should give his fellow human being the space to develop, instead of crushing him against the wall. Humility is the labor of the love that is put into practice, the love that the opening verses called a divine gift (Phil 2:1) and a human task (Phil 2:2). It breaks through the *bellum omnium contra omnes*, the "war of all against all," the compulsion to outdo one another, and the conflicts to which this leads. By giving the central place to the peace of God (Phil 2:2; 4:7) instead of selfishness and contentiousness (*eritheia*), it is in accordance with the "God of peace" (Phil 4:9).

In view of the misunderstandings and the erroneous interpretation that we have sketched above, it cannot be too strongly insisted that such humility has nothing in common with a calculating or neurotic abasement of the "I": its concern is rather to raise up the "thou," as the apostle very pointedly says at 2 Corinthians 11:7 with regard to the community that is humiliating him.[47] The goal is the preservation of the unity of the community: "unity through humility."[48] Humility is thus a striking example of how the orientation to Christ leads in Paul to a new orientation of ethics in substantial terms too.[49]

Verse 4 underlines this yet again by making a provocative demand that directly contradicts the instinct for self-preservation that is inherent in every living being and the self-interest that is linked to this: "let each of you look not to his own interests, but also to the interests of others." The "also" (*kai*) is omitted in a number of manuscripts, which however do not all belong to the most important category.

This deletion shows that it was considered necessary to correct Paul's affirmations to make him a spokesman for total selflessness. This, however, is not what the apostle actually says. Rather, "due attention shall be paid to one's own interests and to those of the others . . . jointly; it is only this that produces a universal harmony."[50]

On verse 5. The apostle is all too well aware of how greatly this conflicts with the being of the old Adam. Is it then too much to require humility of this human being? No, provided that it is made clear at the same time how believers are enabled to behave in this way. In order to do this, the apostle "pulls out all the stops," so to speak, when he coins anew the concept of humility. He quotes in justification an entire hymn (something unparalleled in his other Letters) that one can understand, in a certain sense, as a kind of counterhistory to the narrative of the fall: whereas the first Adam wants to be like God and thereby loses paradise, the "last Adam" (a name that Paul gives to Christ at 1 Cor 15:45; cf. 1 Cor 15:20-22) renounces his divinity and attains, through his self-abasement, a unique fellowship with God and a sublime dignity.

When Paul introduces this hymnic passage with the exhortation to have the mind that corresponds to existence in Christ, this "having the mind" (*phronein*) alludes to the earlier twofold *phronein* (being of the same mind, being intent upon being one) in verse 2 and to *tapeinophrosunê*, "being intent upon that which is lowly," in other words, "humility." At the same time, this verse points to what is to come, namely, to the hymn that shows that humility is a disposition that accords with existence in Christ.

A moralizing misunderstanding of this verse, and of the entire text with it, would limit it to the imitation of Christ as model. The interpretation as a pure *imitatio Christi* dominated the exegesis of Philippians 2 for a long time; it is still found in the NRSV: "Let the same mind be in you that was in Jesus Christ." But, as E. Käsemann has shown, such a translation is at least one-sided, if not in fact misleading.[51] For "in Christ," the phrase that was already used in verse 1 and is repeated here in verse 5, is a standard formula in Paul and is characteristic of his theology. It occurs eight times in Philippians alone[52] and expresses the integration of believers into a new system of relationships that is defined by Christ. "In Christ" indicates a new location, so to speak, into which the believers are transposed, the heavenly city as a sphere of salvation and life (*politeuma*, Phil 3:20), which constitutes a sphere of relationship and of power[53] that even now leaves its mark on the believers in such a way[54] that Paul can say that Christ is life for him (Phil 1:21) and that the believers too should lead a life as citizens [of heaven] (*politeuesthe*) that is worthy of the Gospel of Christ (Phil 1:27). This means that a change of subject takes place "in Christ," and Paul can use striking language at Galatians 2:20 to express this: "it is no longer I who live, but it is Christ who lives in me."[55] Indeed, the apostle can employ at 2 Corinthians 5:17 the category of a new creation to express the radicality of the new constitution of existence that results from this: "if anyone [is] in Christ: new creation." This transformation through the transfer into a new context of life[56] has immediate consequences not only for the relationship to God but also for the relationship to one's neighbor. For the hymn tells the story of this life of another (namely, Christ), which becomes one's own story "in Christ" in such a way that the love received in Christ's gift of self becomes the basis of a new life praxis, which is oriented to Christ's conduct and is shaped by it[57]—this is the element of truth in an exegesis that underlines the exemplary quality of Christ here. For otherwise, Paul could have been content with the phrase "in Christ"; it would not have been necessary for him to quote the entire hymn about Christ. Paul often posits this correspondence between Christ's salvific activity (*sacramentum*) and his exemplary quality (*exemplum*) in other passages:

> Each of you must please his neighbor . . .
> For Christ did not please himself. (Rom 15:2-3)
>
> Welcome one another, therefore,
> just as Christ has welcomed you, for the glory of God.
> (Rom 15:7; cf. also 2 Cor 10:11)

K. Backhaus sums it up correctly:

> Christ predisposes . . . in a comprehensive manner the *basis of life*, since the believer lives in and from the fellowship with Christ (I), the *goal of life*, since Christ gives their ultimate end to the spheres within which ethical conduct moves (II), and the *criterion of life*, since ethical existence under the conditions of the old aeon is permanently directed to the reference to Christ (III). In short, Christ shapes the "with," the "for," and the "between" of the ethical existence.[58]

In order to understand the hymn, it is helpful to realize how unusual is the way it refers to the Christ event only a few years after Jesus' death.[59] For the language about a preexistent divine figure who divested himself of his divinity and took on human form to the uttermost consequence, namely, to death on the cross, and who then, in return, was exalted by God into the highest heights, so that now everything in heaven and on earth and under the earth confesses him as *Kyrios*, is anything but a simple retelling of the story of Jesus that is transmitted in the Gospels. Rather, the hymn practically omits the earthly activity of Jesus[60] and concentrates on the themes of preexistence, self-emptying, incarnation, exaltation, and enthronement at the right hand of God. In other words, it transmits the Christ event with the help of mythical motifs (*mythemes*). A great variety of attempts have been made in New Testament exegesis to identify more precisely the origin of the mythemes employed here in Old Testament, Jewish, pagan, or even gnostic sources.[61] One would have to investigate how much of this applies to this text: Should we assume that its background is one single, clearly defined tradition, or is the hymn an independent composition that synthesizes "various ideas in a religious-historical, syncretistic manner,"[62] referring to them, surpassing them, or attacking them? There is some evidence that the hymn alludes by way of antithesis to the imperial cult,[63] and this would serve only to confirm our interpretation of the hymn about Christ in the context of a discourse about status and power. Here, however, it is not primarily the origin of the individual mythical elements that is important, but their function. This is first and foremost christological: the life story of the Galilean carpenter Jesus of Nazareth, who was executed by the Roman governor Pontius Pilatus in ca. 30 CE as a politically suspect messianic pretender, was marginal in terms of world history, but the mythemes mentioned above are employed to locate it in a context that far surpasses his appearance on the scene of history. What happened to Jesus is thus already interpreted, a few years after his death, as an event that comes from the eternity of God and flows into this eternity—and the consequence is a revolution that encompasses heaven, the earth, and the underworld. This is why this hymn was from the very beginning one of the most important New Testament texts for the development of Christology (which, as Hengel observes, went further in these first years after Jesus' death than in the following seven centuries until the Christology of the early church was fully developed).[64]

On verses 6-8. In the first strophe, we are told that Christ did not hold fast to his "divine mode of being."[65] In other words, he did not exploit it for himself but took the apparently senseless path of a voluntary "metamorphosis" from the *morphê theou* to the *morphê doulou.* By describing this as a self-emptying, the hymn makes it clear that this "change of form" does not remain something merely external: rather, Christ gives up "something fundamental."[66] This path of expropriation leads to the uttermost point of wretchedness of the *conditio humana*, which is understood as *douleia* (cf. Gal 4:3), namely, the death of a slave on the cross. The word *tapeinoun* has a key function here. In the hymn, it designates Christ's self-abasement; in the paraenesis, it justifies the *tapeinophrosunê*, the humility that is demanded of the believers, on the basis of their having "the form of Christ."[67] In this way, the lexical field *tapeinos* links the hymn with the paraenesis, and it is possible that the hymn, by employing the verb *tapeinoun* for the path of Christ, suggested to the apostle—who was certainly familiar with the negative connotations of this lexical family—in combination with his demand for a renewal of the mind (*phronein*), the new interpretation of the word *tapeinophrosunê*, which was to have such momentous consequences.

On verses 9-11. This was possible only because the abasement and expropriation did not end in the nothingness of death but led to the tremendous plenitude and sovereignty of the crucified Jesus. The reason for this sovereignty is that, at the point where the protagonist of the first half, the Jesus who abases himself, definitively meets his end, another subject appears, namely God. This new actor, to whom the first part of the hymn had referred at most indirectly, by speaking of the obedience of the one who abased himself, now takes charge, so to speak, and brings about the reversal of Jesus' fate. This reversal is a divine proof of the divine power—but a proof of power that is in accordance with what we have said above about the empowering power of God.

In order to understand the radicality of this reversal that God brings about, and hence also its explosiveness, we must realize that the divine exaltation of which the hymn sings does not merely consist in the reestablishing of the original state of things so that, at the end, Christ would simply clothe himself anew in the divine form that he had temporarily laid aside.[68] The aim of the divine reaction, which is introduced by a consecutive "therefore" (*dia*), is to exalt the one who was brought low to a height that is far more than the original state of the divine mode of being that is mentioned in verse 6. The first expression of the "exaltation to the Most High" (as one could pointedly translate *huperupsoô*) is the fact that Jesus receives a new name: *Kyrios*. As "the name that is above every name," this can only be God's sacred proper name,[69] the tetragrammaton of the Hebrew Bible, the Septuagint renders as *Kyrios*. The consequence of this handing over of God's sacred proper name to Jesus is that now, "in the name of Jesus, every knee should bend, of things in heaven and on earth and under the earth, and every tongue should confess: The Lord [is] Jesus Christ." This is an allusion to Isaiah 45:23 LXX, where, however, it is God to whom homage is paid[70] (and the apostle himself refers this prophetic text to God at Romans 14:11, where he quotes it verbatim). If Jesus now receives God's own name, and an honor is paid thereby to him that is owed to God (and only to God) in the Old Testament pre-text, this means nothing less than that the one who has made the total gift of himself in obedience is enthroned by God as ruler of the universe and is acclaimed as *Kyrios* by those in heaven, those on earth, and those under the earth—that is to say, by the representatives of the tripartite cosmos.

Everything is thus oriented to the dramatic revolutions that are brought about by the descent and the ascent. These revolutions concern not only Christ and the cosmos but God as well, since the "sovereignty of the 'one who descends,'"[71] which is described in the second strophe of the hymn, and the "[paradoxical] career" of the one who is brought low[72] are possible only through the action of the God who has hitherto borne the "name that is above every name" and who now hands over this name to the one who had been brought low together with the (total) power that is linked to this name. But such a handing over of the name means that God, for his part, has not insisted on retaining his divine uniqueness as the "one Lord," the *kyrios heis*, that the central Jewish confession, the *Shema Yisrael*, confesses him to be (Deut 6:4 LXX).

And this is how Paul understood it, as we see from his christological reformulation of the *Shema* at 1 Corinthians 8:6, a parallel confession of God the Father as the origin and goal of all things and of Christ as the mediator of the creation and the new creation ("we through him"):

> But for us [there is] one God, the Father [*heis ho theos ho patêr*],
> from whom [are] all things and for whom we [are],
> and one Lord, Jesus Christ [*heis Kyrios Iêsous Khristos*],
> through whom [are] all things, and we [exist] through him.

Through handing over his name, including the power linked to that name, God has thus expropriated himself by making the crucified Jesus his coregent. This is expressed above all in the idea of the *sessio ad dexteram*, which has an extraordinarily wide attestation in the New Testament.[73] To put it exaggeratedly and somewhat provocatively, God himself does exactly what Paul's paraenesis has just demanded of the believers in connection with humility. God does not look to his own interests but regards the other as higher than himself.[74] Since, of course, Jesus has done nothing out of his own resources but owes his exaltation exclusively to what God has done to him, the lordship and the rule of Christ do not in any way call into question the uniqueness of the biblical God, which is once again explicitly emphasized, two verses previously.[75]

If humility is to be related not only to the Jesus who abases himself but also to the God who gives a share in his own power and sovereignty and thus exalts the other, it can no longer be interpreted in exclusively negative terms as a renunciation of status that was rewarded by God with exaltation (as a reward for the believer's deference, so to speak). Existence in Christ means fellowship with the God who gives a share in his own sovereignty to the one who has abased himself, and this fellowship proves its worth precisely in self-restraint on behalf of others. This is why the concluding phrase "to prove the glory of God [as] the Father" is more than a mere "doxological closing formula."[76] This phrase, which many commentators regard as a composition by the apostle,[77] forms the goal at which the entire hymn in its present form aims: "in brief but typically Pauline fashion, this phrase brings the whole argument under the heading of the greater glory of God."[78] It is scarcely by chance that this is the first passage in which God is called "Father." Just as Christ receives *Kyrios*, the old name of God, as his new name, so too God receives a new name. The divine epithet "Father," which is largely avoided in the Old Testament, now becomes his proper name. Indeed, God displays his *doxa*, the power of his glory that shines forth into this world, precisely by the fact that, as Father, he exalts Christ and imparts his divinity and power to the Son. The fatherhood of God corresponds to the new lordship of Christ. God does not want to be the Most High on his own, and he exalts his counterpart above all things: this is now his honor and his glory.[79] This is the real meaning of the name "Father" in the New Testament.[80]

The believers are integrated "in Christ" into this event of the reciprocal expropriation and glorification in which Christ becomes the *Kyrios* and God becomes the Father. Since the *Kyrios Khristos* who is exalted in this way becomes the Lord of the believers and the Father of Jesus Christ thereby also becomes their Father, the exaltation also includes those who are "in Christ" and thus become God's sons or children (Phil 2:15).[81] The promise of exaltation that is implicit here recalls the beatitudes of Jesus (Luke 6:20-21 par. Matt 5:3ff.), and Paul himself expresses it explicitly elsewhere with the help of the category of the "inheritance" that is a consequence of being children of God (Gal 4:6-7; Rom 8:15-17). It may therefore rightly be called the "implicit soteriology of the hymn,"[82] which is made explicit in the promise at Philippians 3:21 that "the body of our lowliness" will be shaped in the likeness of Christ's "body of glory."

The hymn in Philippians thus makes it clear that the deepest foundation of humility is the fellowship with Christ who abases himself[83] and, through him, with the God who displays his glory as Father by renouncing his exclusive sovereignty.[84] According to Jesus' teaching, the only one who will enter the kingdom of God is the one who receives it like a child (Mark 10:15); similarly, the promise of exaltation holds good for the humble person, as the child of God. In return, the demand can be made that one continually put aside "in Christ" the obsession with one's own interests, in favor of the other person. Indeed, this is the only appropriate mode of behavior, which allows the humble person to reflect the "consolation from love," the "sharing in the Spirit," and the "compassion and sympathy" that are established in the community "in Christ" (Phil 2:1) and to become thereby a brother and sister to one's fellow human beings (Phil 1:12; 3:1.23, 27; 4:1; cf. 1:14; 4:21). This is why Paul can say, following the hymn, that the believers, as children of God, shine in the cosmos like stars (Phil 2:15; cf. Matt 5:15-16).

Although the apostle does not employ the word *tapeinophrosunê* in his other Letters, humility is a frequent theme, most clearly in the paraenesis of the Letter to the Romans, where he once again takes up his reflections in Philippians 2. The use of the words *tapeinos* and *phronein* makes it impossible to overlook the semantic echo of *tapeinophrosunê*. Between his exhortations to unity within the community[85] and to renounce vengeance against outsiders,[86] Paul makes this demand:

> Do not be haughty [*mê ta hupsêla phronountes*],
> but give yourselves to humble things [*tois tapeinois*],
> do not think yourselves to be wise [*phronimoi*]. (Rom 12:16b)

The attitude of one who is not presumptuous but finds his orientation in lowliness or in lowly persons is, as it were, the hinge between love of neighbor and love of enemies—an idea that is taken up in the First Letter of Peter (1 Pet 3:8-9).

Before we examine this in detail, let us first look at the Letters that were probably written in his name by pupils of Paul.

The Immediately Pauline School: Letters to the Colossians and the Ephesians

No sooner is the idea of humility introduced than it is abused: the earliest Deutero-Pauline Letter, Colossians, already warns against those who make use of humility to "puff themselves up" (Col 2:18; cf. 2:23). But this abuse did not prevent the Letter to the Colossians from speaking of humility in a perfectly natural way in its paraenesis, as one of the virtues that are essential for the unity of the community:

> [12]As God's chosen ones, holy and beloved,
> clothe yourselves with compassion, kindness, humility,
> meekness, and patience.
> [13]Bear with another and, if anyone has a complaint against
> another,
> forgive each other;
> just as the Lord has forgiven you,
> so you also must forgive.
> [14]Above all, [clothe yourselves] with love,
> which binds everything together in perfect harmony.
> (Col 3:12-14)

Here too humility is based on the gracious action of God: the addressees are called the chosen of God, "holy and beloved." The mutual fellowship based on love is made possible by this gracious action; the collocation of humility and meekness (*praütês*) is strikingly reminiscent of the "Savior's tender invitation" at Matthew 11:29.

The other Deutero-Pauline Letter that, with Colossians, is the most immediate continuation of Pauline tradition takes up the formulations in Colossians but presses them into the service of its central concern, the unity of the church. It begins its paraenesis with a passionate appeal to believers to lead a life that accords with their call (Eph 4:1) by preserving "the unity of the Spirit in the bond of peace" (Eph 4:3). This, however, is possible only

> with all humility and gentleness,
> with patience,
> bearing with one another in love. (Eph 4:2)

One must therefore attach greater importance to fellowship with other Christians than to one's own interests, thereby making possible and preserving the unity of the church. Through humility, gentleness, and patience—the virtues familiar to us from the Letter to the Colossians, which are understood here too as concretions of love (Eph 4:2b)—believers live in accordance with the one God, who is himself one in the fellowship of Father, Son, and Spirit. This is set out in verses 4-6 through the deliberate interweaving of divine and human unity:

> One body and one Spirit,
> just as you were called to the one hope of your calling,
> one Lord, one faith, one baptism,
> one God and Father of all,
> who is above all and through all and in all.

This makes it clear that, just as God is not "one" in the sense of a monad but One in the differentness of Father, Son, and Spirit, so too the triune God reaches out to the community and manifests itself as a unifying force precisely by creating unity in the community.[87] This idea of a unity of God in the differentness of Father, Son, and Sprit, which precisely in this way binds the many together to form one body, is a development of ideas that occur in the New Testament for the first time in Paul, at 1 Corinthians 12:4-11. In Paul, the concrete issue is the one single origin of the manifold gifts, which makes those endowed with these gifts members of one single body; the Letter to the Ephesians emphasizes more strongly, through the sevenfold "one" (Eph 4:4-6), "being one" as a characteristic of the divine and the unifying effect of this "being one" on those who belong to the divine and who participate in the divine unity because they are bound together into *one* body through *one* hope, *one* faith, and *one* baptism. The triad "humility, gentleness, and patience" describes the modes of conduct that correspond to the triune God. These allow the believers, in accordance with their call (Eph 4:1; cf. 4:3), to bear with their fellow human beings in love and thus to realize the "unity[88] of the faith."[89] This is elaborated in the following verses with regard to the variety of the gifts and ministries in the church. The Letter emphasizes here—as it has already done in the introduction to this section, at Ephesians 4:2—that this unity is realized through the building up of the body in love, on which the conclusion to this section twice insists (Eph 4:15-16).

Humility as a Keyword of Christian Ethics: 1 Peter

The First Letter of Peter is the first writing in early Christianity to see humility as the embodiment of the Christian life and to give it a correspondingly prominent place in its paraenesis. Although this probably pseudepigraphical text[90] displays a clear theological independence,[91] it is nevertheless indisputable that it belongs at least in the expanded sphere of the influence of Pauline theology. This can also be seen in the two passages in which 1 Peter speaks of humility. There are numerous allusions and parallels,[92] above all in the first passage, 1 Peter 3:8-9, that confirm the literary dependence of this Letter on Philippians 2 and Romans 12.

Humility is first mentioned in 1 Peter 3:8-9. These two verses form the conclusion of the three directives in which 1 Peter exhorts the Christians to submit "for the Lord's sake" to those who have power over them,[93] so their symbolic existence as "aliens and exiles" may lead the hostile world around them to praise God. The last of these three exhortations to submission, which is addressed to the wives, is followed—probably thanks to the influence of the Haustafel tradition—by an exhortation to the husbands to honor their wives as co-heirs of grace (1 Pet 3:7). This in turn is followed by a general exhortation in two parts. The first part demands unity within the community; the second demands the renunciation of revenge vis-à-vis the external world:

> Finally, all of you,
> have unity of spirit, sympathy, love for one another,
> a tender heart, and a humble mind.
> Do not repay evil for evil or abuse for abuse;
> but, on the contrary, repay with a blessing.
> It is for this that you were called—
> that you might inherit a blessing. (1 Pet 3:8-9)

The adjective *tapeinophrôn*, which occurs only here in the New Testament,[94] echoes the preceding exhortations to submission and thus accords with the orientation to an ethos of submissiveness that is characteristic of 1 Peter. This submission is not a mere bowing to a human authority but is carried out "for the Lord's sake" (1 Pet 2:13) or "in reverence" before God (1 Pet 2:18; 3:2). In this way, it is a testimony of faith in a difficult environment. And this is why humility should not be too quickly confused with servility here.[95] In the first place, humility is not demanded only of those whose social position means that they are in any case inferior. Rather, just as 1 Peter makes slaves in their sufferings models for the entire community,[96] so too it makes humility the distinguishing mark of all Christians. Second, what is involved here (as Paul has already stated in Phil 2 and Rom 12) is not a self-diminution but a mutual consideration that allows love to take on a concrete form. This is why L. Goppelt in his commentary translates the adjective *tapeinophrôn* rather freely, but not inappropriately, as "courteous."[97]

It is surely not by chance that humility is located in 1 Peter 3:8 (like its equivalent in Rom 12) precisely between the exhortations to have unity within the community and to renounce vengeance vis-à-vis outsiders.[98] This hinge position indicates the special place that humility has in Christian conduct, which is further confirmed by the exhortation that closes the Letter. In 1 Peter 3:8, as in Paul and the Deutero-Pauline texts, the exhortation to humility is accompanied by other corresponding exhortations, but in the two verses 1 Peter 5:5-6, in which the Letter employs the word group *tapeinos ktl.* three times, humility becomes the exclusive "basis of contact among Christians."[99]

This concluding exhortation is also concerned with power and subordination. It is immediately preceded by the demand that those who are "younger" should submit to the "elders" (1 Pet 5:5a).[100] But this exhortation in turn is the appendix to a much longer warning to the elders that they are not to abuse their power and to the appeal to tend the flock as imitators of Christ "the chief shepherd," bearing responsibility before God.[101] First Peter warns appositely against "oppression" (*katakurieuein*). This word is relatively rare in Greek[102] and should probably be understood as an allusion to Jesus' logion about reciprocal service as behavior that contrasts with oppression by the powerful (Mark 10:42-45 par. Matt 20:25-28).

First Peter 5:1-5a concludes with a summary that sees in humility the conduct that unites all the members of the community: "all of you must clothe yourselves with humility in your dealings with one another" (1 Pet 5:5b). Once again, the exhortation to humility is addressed to everyone, including those in high positions. This reciprocity in humility is important, so that it may not be misunderstood as a continuation of the directives about submission and thus as the religious consolidation of societal hierarchies; 1 Peter is certainly aware of the potential injustice of such hierarchies (cf. 1 Pet 2:18-20).

The metaphorical expression "clothe yourselves with humility" evokes the association of the slave's apron and emphasizes that an effort is needed if one is to live the alternative to the "natural" tendency to get one's own way. But humility is not only the basis of conduct toward other people. When 1 Peter quotes Proverbs 3:34 in the Septuagint version at 1 Peter 5:5c,

> for God opposes the proud,
> but gives grace to the humble,

humility is located in a direct relationship to God, in a double sense. First, this quotation means that "these are the criteria of God himself, which now provide orientation for the readers,"[103] and that ultimately these are the criteria that decide God's relationship to them. Second, the following verse underlines once again the attitude that this scriptural text counsels and the promise it contains. The author begins with a resumptive *oun* and explains the antithetical *parallelismus membrorum* of the scriptural text through a synthetic *parallelismus membrorum* of his own:

> Humble yourselves therefore under the mighty hand of God,
> so that he may exalt you in due time. (1 Pet 5:6)

We may be inclined to follow L. Goppelt in seeing this exhortation in relation to the Christians' situation in society and in interpreting it as a call to accept their fate, since "it is not only human blindness and wickedness that [are] at work in the harassments and injuries that are inflicted on the Christians because they are Christians . . . but God, in judgment and in grace."[104] There are other scholars who read this passage in a similar way,[105] and this interpretation doubtless contains a particle of truth, since the acceptance of God's will is a concern that runs throughout the entire Letter (cf. 1 Pet 4:19). But this reading places the accent too one-sidedly on submission to the power of the God who is at present experienced as a hidden God. First Peter is familiar with God's hiddenness (1 Pet 1:8) and knows of the inner trial caused by the suffering that is permitted by God (1 Pet 4:12), but the author's answer is that this gives the believers a share in Christ's sufferings (1 Pet 4:13-16). In 1 Peter, God's power is not on the side of those who cause the Christians' sufferings. Rather, it is praised in the doxologies as an empowering,[106] countervailing power (1 Pet 5:10-11; cf. 4:11). In this passage, therefore, the aphorism is to be read in connection with the preceding quotation, as an invitation and a summons to trust in the God who resists human hubris and thereby cares for his suffering community. This, at any rate, is the meaning of the quotation in 1 Peter.

This also indicates the meaning of the "mighty hand" (v. 6). It is not so much that God is at work even "in harassments and injuries"; a more obvious association is with the "strong hand" with which God, according to the testimony of the Old Testament, liberated his people from servitude (Exod 3:19; 6:1; 13:9; et passim). The main point would therefore be not submission to the will of God but being kept safe[107] by the God who does not leave his people alone "in harassments and injuries," but holds them fast and strengthens them even there (1 Pet 5:10), and who will exalt them at the end. This accords with the tenor of the rest of the Letter, as Elliott rightly notes, "the pattern humility-exaltation replicates the patterns of suffering-glory (1:1; 3:18, 22; 4:13, 14; 5:1, 10) and shame-honor (2:4, 10; 4:14, 16)."[108]

The hymn in Philippians implicitly holds out the prospect of exaltation. The reference here to the God who exalts is an explicit promise to the humble that they will be exalted. At the same time, it underlines that the believer is held fast by God's hand. This caring character of the "strong hand of God" and its significance for the present experience of believers are once again underlined emphatically in the concluding invitation:

> Cast all your anxiety on him,
> because he cares for you. (1 Pet 5:7)

If the "bowing down" under God's mighty hand is understood in this way as an invitation to trust and to cast off one's cares, we can readily grasp why one and the same word field, *tapeinos ktl.*, can designate both the relationship to God and the relationship to one's neighbor in 1 Peter, without equivocation. In each case, "humility" is the expression of a self-limitation that seeks to create a space for an encounter and thus to make fellowship possible. Humility is the bond of love—for God and for one's neighbor.

Self-Diminution as Submission to God: Humility in the Letter of James

The Letter of James emphasizes, even more explicitly than the First Letter of Peter, that the power structures of "above" and "below" are shattered in the presence of God. The Letter inveighs with prophetic fervor against the preferential treatment of the rich and the disregard of the poor, which clearly—despite all the blessings pronounced on the poor and the exhortations to humility—had soon made their way back into the Christian communities (Jas 2:1-9; 5:1-6). James demands humility instead, and this polemical position explains why humility now starkly contrasts the arrogance that is linked especially to riches.

This is already indicated at the beginning of the Letter, where the reversal of high and low, which is promised in the words of Jesus, takes the form of a direct call to the believers:

> Let the lowly brother [*ho adelphos ho tapeinos*] boast in highness,
> and the rich in lowliness [*en tê[i] tapeinôsei*],
> because he will disappear like a flower in the field. (Jas 1:9-10)

It is striking that the Letter of James does not contrast the rich with the poor here but with the lowly, probably because, "as the Old and New Testaments understand it, the lowly person is permitted in a particular way to expect that God will act in his favor."[109] This is also the reason for the praise of the lowly person, since—as James 2:5 puts it, echoing the blessing pronounced on the poor in the Sermon on the Plain (Luke 6:20)—"God has chosen the poor in the world to be rich in faith and heirs of the kingdom." Likewise, the lowly person is not contrasted with the one who is on high but with the rich, although these two terms almost become synonymous. Exegetes disagree about what the praise of the rich person means. If one does not add the word "brother" to the rich man and thus understands in a negative sense the "lowliness" of which he is to boast as his transience that is described in the following words, the problem is "that the boasting of the two is not really analogous."[110] The affirmation is more consistent if the rich man too is a "brother" and his lowliness means a "lowliness before God"[111] on which he is to rely alone. This would mean that the attitude of humility is already recommended here.

The Letter speaks explicitly of humility in its fourth chapter. At the end of the third chapter, a contrast is drawn between earthly wisdom and the "wisdom from above" (Jas 3:17; cf. 3:15) that finds expression in kindness and mercy and that brings about peace. The latter point is emphasized by the threefold use of *eirênê ktl.* James 4 now asks why strife and contention nevertheless exist in the community. The starting point here too is thus the perspective of the community: the peace in question is peace in the community, and this ecclesial dimension is not unimportant for the theme of humility, which the Letter now takes up.

The Letter identifies clearly the source of the conflict. The causes are not external but internal, and the disagreement comes from "the desires that are at war in your members"

(Jas 4:1). The author wrote at 1:15 that desire (*epithumia*) gives birth to sin, and sin gives birth to death. Here, he states that pleasure and desire (*hêdonê*, *epithumein*) leave the human being unsatisfied in his depths, thus depriving him of peace and making him destructive both for himself and for the community.[112] These desires, which are unquenchable and thus boundless, have a cause of their own: they are rooted in a love for the world that is the reverse side of enmity vis-à-vis God (4:4). For James, therefore, human beings lack peace because they are "adulterers" (4:4) who have deserted God to pursue another love, love for the "world."[113]

The essentially theocentric perspective of the argumentation is expanded in verse 5 with a reference to God's own "feeling": "the scripture says"—according to James[114]—that God "yearns jealously for the spirit that he has made to dwell in us." This probably refers to the spirit that God gave the human being at creation as the breath of life.[115] The Letter goes on to state in verse 6a, linked to verse 5 by an adversative *de* (but), that God, who has not only created the human being but has promised the crown of life to those who love him (cf. Jas 1:12), surpasses even the creation by giving grace all the more richly.[116] The author explains this by means of the aphorism at Proverbs 3:34 LXX, which is widely attested in early Judaism and early Christianity:[117] "God opposes the proud, but gives grace to the humble."

This quotation once again introduces the concept of lowliness or humility, which is central to the following passage. *Tapeinos* designates quite simply the attitude that is antithetical to arrogance. Just as arrogance is equivalent to resisting God, so humility is the appropriate human attitude vis-à-vis God, who rewards it with loving care. Humility is thus the condition for receiving "grace all the more richly." This is stated first as an obligation, and then as a promise. The obligation demands that one submit to God and resist the devil:

> Submit yourselves therefore to God.
> Resist the devil,
> and he will flee from you. (Jas 4:7)

The submission and the resistance interlock, as two sides of the same coin. We then read about the effect that the Letter of James, with a considerable measure of optimism,[118] presupposes in the addressees: while the devil flees from those who resist him, God draws near to those who draw near to him:

> Draw near to God,
> and he will draw near to you. (Jas 4:8a)

We are then told how one draws near to God. The introductory imperative at 4:7, "submit yourselves"—an attitude that this Letter demands only with regard to God, not to human authorities inside or outside the community—is now explicated as a sanctification and purification that counter the attempt to be a friend both of God and of the world[119] by a "summons to undivided obedience, as the address 'double-minded' (cf. 1:8) shows":[120]

> Cleanse your hands, you sinners,
> and purify your hearts, you double-minded.[121]
> Lament and mourn and weep.
> Let your laughter be turned into mourning
> and your joy into dejection.
> Humble yourselves before the Lord,
> and he will exalt you. (Jas 4:8b-9)

Humility is demanded because it is in conformity with the God who has chosen the poor (2:5) and exalts them (1:9) but who resists the arrogant (4:5) and judges the rich (5:16). The promise of God's closeness concludes the first three imperatives in the section 4:7-8a, and the following seven imperatives in 4:8b-9 culminate in the promise of exaltation. With these two promises of God's closeness and of exaltation, the Letter tells us the meaning of the "even richer gift of grace" (4:6) that God bestows on the humble.

Unlike the texts about humility that we have discussed earlier and unlike Jesus' directives about service, the central ground is no longer occupied by the idea of a positive correspondence to Christ's gift of self out of love for one's neighbor and by being held fast in God's caring power. The central idea here is a radical self-diminution as submission to God.[122] The demand that one weep instead of laugh and that joy be transformed into mourning may perhaps be not the renunciation of all laughter and joy but only a criticism of the "laughter of the godless fool."[123] Nor can we overlook the allusion to logia of Jesus such as Luke 6:21 and 25. Above all, the self-diminution has a positive goal here, namely, the realization of love and of peace in the fellowship. This is already demonstrated by the beginning of the passage James 4:1-2, and the following verses, 4:11-12, underline it once again.

Nevertheless, as we have already indicated, the idea of humility in the Letter of James has a darker tone, because it is a critique of human arrogance to a much sharper degree than appears in the texts we have discussed earlier. It is easy to grasp the meaning of the demand for self-abasement in the "prophetic penitential sermon"[124] of the Letter of James, which passionately upholds the rights and the dignity of the poor (cf. Jas 1:9; 2:4-6) and correspondingly criticizes the rich and the arrogant (cf. Jas 1:10-11; 2:5-7; 4:13-17; 5:1-16) and those Christians who pay court to them (2:1-9). But if the words we have quoted are detached from their context, humility means the renunciation of all joy in life and becomes a synonym for a pathological negation of life. This is how it was possible to arrive at the distortion of the idea of humility that we sketched at the beginning of the present chapter, in the sense of a sectarian obsessiveness that is widely attested in the use of this term[125] and that turns the life-affirming character of this attitude into its opposite.

But despite all the possibility of distortion and abuse—which have occurred again and again—the ideal of humility remains central to Christianity. Christian movements such as monasticism or Protestant social welfare have made their own this aspect of *humilitas* as a way of life, in the attempt to live a project that runs contrary to the societal power structures and to a church that repeatedly reproduces these structures. This project provokes hierarchical thinking and calls it into question in a more elementary manner than every rebellion that itself remains attached to the paradigm of power. Let us emphasize once more, with regard to the question of power, that such projects were far from powerless. On the contrary, they attained a beneficial influence on church and society.[126]

Accordingly, in his *Recommendation of Humility*, the late mediaeval mystic Thomas à Kempis emphasizes the salutary power of humility:

> Through humility, atonement is made to God for all offenses, the neighbor who is hurt in any way is strengthened, the devil is put to shame, heaven is opened to the sinner, and every crime is expiated. . . . For humility alone escapes all the snares of the Devil and vanquishes his power.[127]

Chapter 4

Once Again: Power

As we have shown, it is possible to read the entire New Testament as the story of a power struggle between a destructive autonomous power that is called mythologically the devil, anthropologically the flesh, and theologically sin, on the one hand, and the good news of the rule of God, on the other hand, which does good to its counterpart, saves, redeems, builds up, endows with gifts, and is thus perfected as a "spiritual," empowering power in the weak.

Jesus of Nazareth bore witness to the presence of this rule of God in his authoritative speaking and acting, which were God's activity through him in favor of the "weary and heavy-laden," and in his powerless suffering and dying as trust in God's activity in him in favor of "the many." This is why both his life and his suffering can be subsumed under the category of service. For the Gospels, Christ is the "Lord" as the one who serves those who belong to him. Paul writes that Christ, as the one who lowered himself and took on the form of a slave, is constituted by God the Father as *Kyrios* over the entire cosmos.

Since those who follow him owe their life to Jesus' gift of himself in service and since they are "a new creation" as believers who live "in Christ," they are not only obligated by the example of Jesus to a different kind of conduct. Rather, they are also enabled to do so in the fellowship "in Christ" that is established through his gift of self, because, as the exalted Lord, he is "in their midst," because his Spirit "dwells" in them and "drives" them—and because the God who has drawn near through him as "Father" "gives" them "all things."

As "servants of the Lord Jesus Christ," therefore, they are likewise children and heirs of God the Father, and thus they are free. When they are urged to adopt an attitude and a behavior of reciprocal service, which does not begin with the "I" but thinks on the basis of the "thou," the goal is thus not self-denial but self-realization as a life together with God and with the neighbor.

Dietrich Bonhoeffer says that "the God of the Bible" is the God "who through his powerlessness gains power and space in the world."[1] The one who serves, the one who is humble, corresponds to this God and has a share in God's spiritual power. As M. Bockmuehl observes, "Humility has in that sense an 'ex-centric' orientation, taking its focus outside oneself, and finding its power in the power of God."[2] Or, to refer back once again, with words of Mother Teresa, to the scene of the temptation of Jesus with which we began this book: "If there is one [*sic*] virtue that terrifies the Devil, it is humility and compassion."[3]

Notes

1 See H. Thielicke, *Zwischen Gott und Satan: Die Versuchung Jesu und die Versuchlichkeit des Menschen*, Wuppertal 1968, 34: "His craving to be like God, his immoderate hunger to be 'equal in rank' to God, which is not content with the mere likeness and with being the 'image' of God—that is what caused the catastrophe."

2 Bernard of Clairvaux, *De consideratione ad Eugenium papam*, 3.1.2: "nam nullum tibi venenum, nullum gladium plus formido, quam libidinem dominandi."

3 I follow here the account given by Matthew, because, as I shall show, the question of power plays a particularly important role in this Gospel.

4 The Matthean narrative is a combination of the brief note in Mark 1:12-13 and the dialogue that comes from the Logia source. It has a parallel in the Gospel of Luke (Luke 4:1-13).

5 In the temptation narrative, the Gospel employs the word *latreuô*, which is found in the LXX and has unambiguously religious connotations (see Luke 1:74; 2:37; Acts 7:7, 42; 24:14; 26:7; 27:23; Rom 1:9, 25; Phil 3:3; and many other passages). The word *diakonein* denotes more strongly the service of one's fellow human beings (see below).

6 This form is typical of the first Gospel, which thereby establishes a relationship between the Scripture and the life of Jesus, demonstrating that this life fulfills the Scripture.

7 A. Schlatter, "Jesu Demut, ihre Missdeutungen, ihr Grund," *BFChTh* 8, Gütersloh 1904, 82.

8 Schlatter, "Demut," 37.

9 Matt 4:17, 23 par. Mark 1:15; cf. Luke 4:16ff.

10 A changeover of power like this is mentioned not only in messianic prophecies such as Isa 9:1-6 and 11:1-16, but also in texts such as Ps 75:11.

11 W. Foerster, art. "*exestin ktl.*," *ThWNT* 2 (1935): 559.

12 See the programmatic logion at Matt 3:15, which the evangelist has introduced into the scene of the baptism.

13 See W. Brandt, *Dienst und Dienen im Neuen Testament* (NTF [Reihe 2] Untersuchungen zum Kirchenproblem des Urchristentums 3), Gütersloh 1931.

14 K. Backhaus, "Evangelium als Lebensraum. Christologie und Ethik bei Paulus," in U. Schnelle, T. Söding, and M. Labahn, eds. *Paulinische Christologie: Exegetische Beiträge* (Festschrift H. Hübner), Göttingen 2000, 21. Backhaus' remarks about Paul are confirmed by J. Roloff with regard to the Gospels: "Jesus appears here as the one who through his conduct shatters the structural principle of dominion and violence, by positing instead of this the principle of an existence in service for others. But he does not remain alone in his serving. Thanks to their close fellowship with Jesus, the disciples are drawn into his conduct, which takes on a prototypical significance for them." Roloff, *Die Kirche im Neuen Testament* (NTD Ergänzungsreihe 10), Göttingen 1993, 41.

Chapter 1

1 See U. von Wilamowitz-Moellendorff, *Der Glaube der Hellenen*. Vol. 1, Darmstadt 1976, 19.

2 S. R. F. Price, "Gods and Emperors. The Greek Language of the Roman Imperial Cults," *Journal of Hellenic Studies* 104 (1984): 86: "Zeus *can* also operate as a predicate referring to a certain type of divine power."

3 See J. P. Vernant, *Myth and Thought among the Greeks*, London 1983, 328: "The Greek gods are powers, not persons. Religious thought is a response to the problems of organizing and classifying these powers."

4 Menander of Athens, *Frg.* 257: "to kratoun . . . pan nomizetai theos."

5 Cicero, *De natura deorum* 1.45: "Habet enim venerationem iustam, quicquid excellit."

6 F. Bilabel, "Fragmente aus der Heidelberger Papyrussammlung," *Philologus* 80 (1925): 339. It is significant that the second line continues, "What [is] a king? Godlike."

7 See J. Rüpke, *Die Religion der Römer: Eine Einführung*, 3rd ed., Munich 2006, 13: "Religion was especially present in the political sphere. The senate always met in a room that was defined in sacral terms, a *templum*. Sessions of the senate were opened with the sacrifice of incense offered by the senators who entered the room, and with a small libation of wine."

8 This is how Polybius of Megalopolis sees it in the second century BCE: "The greatest advantage of the Roman polity . . . seems to me to lie in its understanding of the gods, and something that is a matter for accusation in other peoples seems to form the basis of the Roman state: namely, an almost superstitious fear of the gods. It is scarcely possible to imagine the kind of role that religion plays both in private and in public life there, and the fuss that is made about it" (*Historiae*, 6.56.6-8). Cicero comes to a similar conclusion about one hundred years later (*De natura deorum* 2.8), when he explains the superiority of Rome over the other peoples exclusively by reference to the particularly faithful veneration of the gods: "and if we wish to compare our situation with those of foreign peoples, it can be seen that in other areas, we are only equal, or even inferior, to them; but with regard to religion, that is, the veneration of the gods, we are much superior [*multo superiores*] to them." The same picture can be seen in the speech of Caecilius in the *Octavius* of Minucius Felix, written probably at the beginning of the third century of the Common Era: the safety of the state is based on the conscientious exercise of religion (*Oct.* 6.2)—a conviction that is astonishingly impervious to the philosophical skepticism represented by Caecilius.

9 On this, see the remarks by A. Wlosok, *Rom und die Christen: Lateinische Quellentexte zur Auseinandersetzung zwischen Christentum und römischem Staat*, Stuttgart 200, 56ff.; a similar position is taken by G. Alföldy, *Römische Sozialgeschichte*, 4th ed., Wiesbaden 2011, 38: "The intellectual basis of this concept of the state was religion."

10 Accordingly, Price concludes, "the imposition of the conventional distinction between religion and politics obscures the basic similarity between politics and religion: both are ways of systematically constructing power." S. R. F. Price, *Rituals and Power: The Roman Imperial Cult in Asia Minor*, Cambridge 2002 (1984), 247.

11 Rüpke, *Religion*, 77. Rüpke demonstrates how individuals in the late republic and in the imperial period legitimated their own claims to power by associating themselves with particular deities and by giving these deities a greater importance through a new cult or through the monumentality of the site chosen for this cult (84–85).

12 See M. P. Nilsson, *Geschichte der griechischen Religion.* Vol. 1: *Die Religion Griechenlands bis auf die griechische Weltherrschaft* (HAW V,2,1), 3rd ed., Munich 1976, 61: The divine "power is desired, because extraordinary things can be attained with its aid; but it is also dangerous, because it can also inflict harm, and its working is mysterious."

13 See Karl Barth, *Die kirchliche Dogmatik.* Vol. 2: *Die Lehre von Gott,* Zurich 1940 (*KD* 2/1), 587: "As is well known, the oldest professions of faith were content to ascribe this *one* characteristic to God. . . . Clearly, they saw precisely this characteristic as the embodiment of all the others, as their compendium, so to speak" (emphasis original).

14 M. Scheler refers (without an exact reference) to a letter of Madame de Pompadour, who attributes this saying to the French Marshal Tourenne (1611–1675). See M. Scheler, *Der Genius des Krieges und der deutsche Krieg*, 3rd ed., Leipzig 1917, 129. It is interesting that Scheler, who agrees with this saying as a "strict inference from the idea of divine omnipotence," sees the abandonment of the idea of power as a relapse into "a classical-scholarly idea of God that had been made obsolete by Christianity" (130).

15 Cf. also Sir 3:18 LXX; on this question as a whole, see W. Grundmann, art. "*tapeinos ktl.*," *ThWNT* 8 (1969): 6–15.

16 For example, in the Letter of Aristeas, one of the Jewish sages who speaks in the presence of the king of Egypt intensifies the biblical statement "God destroys the arrogant, but he exalts the merciful and humble" (263), after another sage before him has made the equally fundamental utterance that "God, in keeping with his nature, is accustomed to receive the one who humbles himself" (257).

17 There is an allusion to it in the Magnificat (Luke 1:52), and it is quoted in Jas 4:6 and 1 Pet 5:5, as well as in *1 Clem.* 30.2 and Ignatius, *Eph.* 5.3.

18 Hesiod, *Works and Days* 5–8 (trans. Hugh G. Evelyn-White); for further references, see H. Hommel, "Der bald erhöhn, bald stürzen kann," in *Sebasmata: Studien zur antiken Religionsgeschichte und zum frühen Christentum*. Vol. 2 (WUNT 32), Tübingen 1984, 3–9.

19 R. Feldmeier and H. Spieckermann, *God of the Living: A Biblical Theology*, trans. Mark A. Biddle, Waco, Tex., 2011, 157.

20 Ps 34:19 LXX: "tous tapeinous tô[i] pneumati sôsei." The statement at Num 12:3 that Moses was the humblest of all men probably also belongs in this context.

21 In the long form, (*ho*) *kyrios* [*ho theos*] (*ho*) *pantokratôr*, one cannot distinguish unambiguously the adjectival and the substantive use, but the substantive character of *pantokratôr* is obvious here; see M. Bachmann, who calls this an "intrinsically sufficient naming of God." Bachmann, *Göttliche Allmacht und theologische Vorsicht: Zu Rezeption, Funktion und Konnotationen des biblisch-frühchristlichen Gottesepithetons pantokrator* (SBS 188), Stuttgart 2002, 162. This is already indicated in Hebrew (see Feldmeier and Spieckermann, *God*, 156), and it can be seen in other names of God too, such as the designation "Highest" (*hupsistos*), "king" (*basileus*), and "ruler" (*dunastês*), and above all where the tetragrammaton, the specific name of the Old Testament God, is translated as *Kyrios* (Lord).

22 This is emphasized programmatically in 1 Bar 3:1, 4.

23 See Feldmeier and Spieckermann, *God*, 147–99, esp. 173–75.

24 See E. Zenger, "I. Überlieferung und Entstehung des Buches," in E. Zenger, *Das Buch Judit* (JSHRZ 1/6), Gütersloh 1981, 431.

25 See Grundmann, "*tapeinos*," 10: "It is the eternal being of God, who is exalted above all the peoples and above all the heavens, that he, 'our God, who dwells in the height, looks down at that which is lowly,' has mercy on the one who is poor (Ps 112:4-7; cf. also 137:6)."

26 Feldmeier and Spieckermann, *God*, 172.

27 See Feldmeier and Spieckermann, *God*, 173–78.

28 See the hymn to Zeus of the Stoic Cleanthes (*Frg.*, 537).

29 H. G. Liddell and R. Scott, *A Greek-English Lexicon*, ed. H. S. Jones, 9th ed., Oxford 1983, 991: "hold in the hand," "repair," "make good."

30 See Pseudo-Tertullian, *Car. adv. Marc.* 5.202; Ambrosiaster, *QT* 1.2. Augustine states emphatically that the primary translation of *pantokratôr* should be *omnitenens*, so that the "Almighty" is always to be understood also as "the one who holds everything" (*In ev. Ioan.* 106.5; cf. Augustine, *Conf.* 7.15; 11.13; *De gen. litt.* 4.12; 8.26).

31 This refers in the first instance to the exterior lowliness of the Galilean girl, but Mary's reply to the angel—"Here am I, the maidservant of the Lord. Let it be with me according to your word" (Luke 1:38)—already shows that an interior attitude corresponds to this exterior lowliness.

32 Mark 1:14-15 par. Matt 4:17; Luke 11:20 par. Matt 12:28.

33 Mark 13:26-27; 14:62 par.; Luke 21:28; cf. also the parables of growth, Mark 4:26-29, 30-32.

34 In addition to the temptation narrative, which we have expounded above, scenes such as Mark 8:10-13 par. Matt 16:1-4; Luke 11:29-32 par. Matt 12:38-42; and Luke 23:8 show Jesus' rejection of miracles that would accredit him.

35 We should note that, when praise is uttered after Jesus' wonders, it is not Jesus but God who is praised (Mark 2:12 par. Matt 9:8; Luke 5:26; cf. Luke 7:16; Mark 5:19).

36 Luke 4:21. This emphatic "today" occurs repeatedly in Luke and underlines the presence of salvation in Jesus—from the proclamation by the angels to the shepherds that "today the Savior has been born for you" (Luke 2:11) to the promise to the man who is crucified alongside Jesus that "today you will be with me in paradise" (Luke 23:43).

37 The film *Jesus of Montreal* shows emphatically how alternative behavior of this kind quickly turns into a deadly collision with the interests of other people.

38 This is the only time in the New Testament that God's fatherhood and his omnipotence are combined (as the Creed later does), in order to hold fast both to God's care and to his power.

39 See 1 Cor 15:20-28, 35-57; Rom 5:12-21; 8:9-11, 38-39.

40 In Phil 3:20, the apostle employs the image of citizenship in heaven or of the heavenly city for this sphere of power, which is based on the enthronement of Jesus Christ as the *Kyrios* (see below); in Gal 4:26, he employs the image of the heavenly Jerusalem. Despite a certain one-sidedness, Peterson is not completely wrong to emphasize the dimension of civil law and politics in Paul's concept of *ekklêsia*. E. Peterson, *Der erste Brief an die Korinther und Paulus-Studien: Aus dem Nachlass herausgegeben*

von Hans-Ulrich Weidemann (Ausgewählte Schriften 7), Würzburg 2006, 29, 35–36.

41 On these opponents' theology of glory, see U. Schnelle, *Einleitung in das Neue Testament*, 5th ed., Göttingen 2005, 107–8.

42 See 2 Cor 10:10; 11:5-6, 16-21.

43 On the "foolish speech" as a whole, see the enlightening study by U. Heckel, *Kraft in Schwachheit: Untersuchungen zu 2. Kor 10–13* (WUNT 2/56), Tübingen 1995.

44 Paul, the theologian of the cross, was extremely successful in gaining and leading fellow workers. On this, see E. Ebel, "Die Reisebegleiter und Mitarbeiter des Paulus," in O. Wischmeyer, ed. *Paulus: Leben—Umwelt—Werk—Briefe*, 2nd ed., Tübingen 2012, 125: "About fifty persons who are mentioned by name in the Pauline Letters and the Acts of the Apostles are directly called fellow workers (*sunergoi*) of Paul, or can be classified as such."

45 Paul introduces the antihistory at the appropriate moment, when he describes his illness as ultimately a divine measure undertaken to prevent the revelations he has received from making him arrogant (2 Cor 12:6-7).

46 See the beautiful lines by Paul Gerhardt that express this experience:

> Wenn mein Können, mein Vermögen,
> nichts vermag noch helfen kann,
> kommt mein Gott und hebt mir an,
> sein Vermögen beizulegen
> [When my power, my best endeavor
> Cometh to extremity,
> Then my God appears to me,
> With his might comes to deliver.]

J. Kelly, *Paul Gerhardt's Spiritual Songs*, London 1867, 242.

47 This verb is attested prior to Paul only three times, in the Greek translation of the Old Testament: see Liddell and Scott, *Lexicon*, 561–62.

48 Rom 4:20; Phil 4:13. In the New Testament, the Pauline school continues to use this verb: Eph 6:10; 1 Tim 1:12; 2 Tim 2:1; 4:7; cf. Acts 9:22.

49 This empowerment is, of course, the exact opposite of the seizure of power for himself by a dictator like Adolf Hitler, whose seizure of power was completed by the *Ermächtigungsgesetz* (Law of Empowerment) in 1933.

50 See K. Blanchard, J. P. Carlos, and A. Randolph, *The 3 Keys to Empowerment: Release the Power Within People for Astonishing Results*, San Francisco 2001; S. R. Covey, *The 7 Habits of Highly Effective People: Powerful Lessons in Personal Change*, New York, 2004; R. Ambrosino, J. Heffernan, G. Shuttelsworth, and R. Ambrosino, *Social Work and Social Welfare: An Introduction*, Brooks/Cole Empowerment Series, 7th ed., Belmont, Calif., 2012; M. Barnes, *Taking Over the Asylum: Empowerment and Mental Health*, Toronto 1998.

51 A detailed exposition of this text will be found in chapter 3 below, "Humility."

52 On the exception with regard to the unique use of the predicate of omnipotence in Paul, see Feldmeier and Spieckermann, *God*, 184–87.

53 See R. Feldmeier, "Das Lamm und die Raubtiere: Tiermetaphorik und Machtkonzeptionen im Neuen Testament," in R. Gebauer and M. Meiser, eds. *Die bleibende Gegenwart des Evangeliums* (Festschrift O. Merk, MThSt 76), Marburg 2003, 205–11.

54 This is why Jesus' authority meets its boundary in the opposition of those he encounters (cf. Mark 6:5).

Chapter 2

1 T. Söding, *Das Liebesgebot bei Paulus: Die Mahnung zur Agape im Rahmen der paulinischen Ethik* (NTA 26), Münster 1995, 192.

2 When there is a risk of relapse, these earlier bonds can be recalled as a warning (see Gal 4:9).

3 See 1 Thess 1:9; Rom 1:9; 12:1, 11; 16:18. This is why one of the apostle's pupils exhorts the slaves succinctly: "Serve the Kyrios Christ!" (Col 3:24; see also Eph 6:7).

4 See chapter 1 above, "Power."

5 In Romans 7:25, Paul concludes his reflections on the lost state of the human being under the law with a summary that depicts the inner turmoil caused by a double service: "So then, with my mind I am a slave to the law of God, but with my flesh I am a slave to the law of sin." (Many exegetes regard these words as an addition to the original text: see U. Wilckens, *Der Brief an die Römer.* Vol. 2: *Römer 6* [EKK 6/2–11], Neukirchen-Vluyn 1980, 96–97).

6 See Brandt, *Dienst*, 95: "It belongs to the essence of this Lord that those who call themselves his *douloi* are not only his servants, but at the same time *douloi* of the community."

7 In Mark 8:31, this is expressed through the *dei* (he must), and in 9:31 and 10:33 through the use of the *passivum divinum*.

8 On the tradition history of this logion and its relationship to the Jewish and Hellenistic worlds, see O. Wischmeyer, "Herrschen als Dienen—Markus 10,41-45," *ZNW* 90 (1999): 28–44. Wischmeyer shows (against Seeley) that the theme of service is present incipiently in early Jewish writings. She also maintains, with good arguments, that the entire logion Mark 10:42-45 goes back to the historical Jesus.

9 In the early Jewish Mishnah tractate Pesahim 50a, we read that the son of Rabbi Joseph had a dream as he lay in a fever. "When he came to himself, his father said: 'What did you see?' He replied: 'I saw an inverted world, with the higher ones below and the lower ones on high.' He said to him: 'My child, you have seen a true world.'" H. L. Strack and P. Billerbeck, *Kommentar zum Neuen Testament aus Talmud und Midrasch.* Vol. 1: *Das Evangelium nach Matthäus*, 2nd ed., Munich 1956, 250.

10 In that case, they would have asked to recline at table with Jesus. Their request to sit beside him surely envisages a throne.

11 Jesus' first and direct answer to the request (namely, that the two disciples do not know what they are asking for), with his question of whether they can drink his cup and be baptized with his baptism, remains strangely ineffective. The two disciples answer Jesus' question in the affirmative, so that he is compelled to give a new answer and then to react to the indignation of the disciples in a third exchange. It is possible that the first word of Jesus once formed the original conclusion, at least of the first part of the apothegm, in which the request of the sons of Zebedee was answered by the admonishment that the path to the heavenly enthronement follows Jesus in suffering.

12 It is possible that the martyrdom of James (cf. Acts 12:2) meant that Jesus' question should now be answered positively and that his rebuff was thus no longer plausible. In a second exchange, therefore, Jesus holds out the prospect of martyrdom to the two disciples in a *vaticinium ex eventu* (see R. Pesch, *Das Markusevangelium: Einleitung und Kommentar zu Kapitel 8,24–16,20* [HThK 2/2], Freiburg 1977, 154, 159–60), while nevertheless leaving it exclusively to the Father to grant the request.

13 R. Pesch, *Das Markusevangelium: Einleitung und Kommentar zu Kapitel 1,1–8,26* (HThK 2/1), Freiburg 1976, 164.

14 See J. D. G. Dunn, *Jesus Remembered: Christianity in the Making.* Vol. 1, Grand Rapids and Cambridge 2003, 560: "It should

be noted that Jesus apparently did not *dis*courage ambition (to be 'great'); but the greatness he commanded was that of the *servant*."

15 D. Bonhoeffer, *Widerstand und Ergebung: Briefe und Aufzeichnungen aus der Haft* (DBW 8), Munich 1998, 559.

16 Although Isaiah 53 probably stands in the background to this logion, this idea of the gift of one's life is intensified here to take in the ransom that is thereby accomplished. "In Greek and in the LXX, *lutron* means the ransom paid for a life that has been forfeited by guilt. It is paid for a slave or a prisoner of war, or in the form of bail." J. Gnilka, *Das Evangelium nach Markus.* Vol. 2: *Mark 8,27–16,20* (EKK 2/2), Neukirchen-Vluyn 1979, 104.

17 Wischmeyer, "Herrschen," 44.

18 See B. Heininger, "'Politische Theologie' im Markusevangelium. Der Aufstieg Vespasians zum Kaiser und der Abstieg Jesu am Kreuz," in C. Mayer, ed. *Augustinus Ethik und Politik: Zwei Würzburger Augustinus-Studientage. Aspekte der Ethik bei Augustinus (11. Juni 2005). Augustinus und die Politik (24. Juni 2006)* (Cassiciacum 39,4 = Res et signa. Augustinus-Studien 4), Würzburg 2009, 171–201.

19 Roloff, *Kirche*, 217.

20 We see this raising up of the human being by God at the annunciation of the birth of Jesus, when Mary, as "the handmaid of the Lord," submits to what God decrees concerning her (Luke 1:38) and then praises God in the Magnificat because "he has looked on the lowliness of his maidservant" (1:48) and has thus revealed himself as the one who has lifted up the lowly (1:52).

21 This exhortation follows the parables about the order of precedence at a meal (Luke 14:7-11) and about the Pharisee and the tax collector (18:9-14).

22 The form is a *passivum divinum*, the Jewish circumlocution that describes the activity of God. Accordingly, it is God himself who will do this.

23 On this, see M. Konradt, "Gott oder Mammon. Besitzethos und Diakonie im frühen Christentum," in C. Sigrist, *Diakonie und Ökonomie: Orientierung im Europa des Wandels* (Beiträge zu Theologie, Ethik und Kirche 1), Zurich 2006, 108–33.

24 M. Konradt, "'Whoever humbles himself like this child . . .' The Ethical Instruction in Matthew's Community Discourse (Matt 18) and Its Narrative Setting," in R. Zimmermann and J. G. v.d. Watt, eds. *Moral Language in the New Testament: The*

Interrelatedness of Language and Ethics in Early Christian Writings. Vol. 2, WUNT (Reihe 2) 296, Tübingen 2010, 137.

25 Konradt, "Instruction," 111.

26 See R. Schnackenburg, *Die sittliche Botschaft des Neuen Testaments*. Vol. 1: *Von Jesus zur Urkirche* (HThK.S 1), Freiburg i.B. 1986, 205: "For John, the washing of the feet points to the gift that Jesus will make of his life (13:7-8)."

27 For example, in the shepherd discourse, the Johannine Jesus directly links the laying down of his life for those who are his and the mutual knowledge of the Father and the Son: "I am the good shepherd. The good shepherd lays down his life for the sheep. . . . Just as the Father knows me and I know the Father. And I lay down my life for the sheep" (10:11, 15).

28 Martin Kähler has impressively described this impact of Jesus' greatness in serving: "He was never engaged in great affairs, but in the indefatigable, faithful small business of life. I, at least, see his royal exaltation perhaps best of all when I see how he remains attached to this small business, without inner turmoil, without pettiness, without losing heart; for it is precisely this small business that makes such infinite claims on him, that he seems to his companions to be going beyond his own strength." Kähler, "Der Menschensohn und seine Sendung an die Menschheit," in H. Frohnes, ed. *Martin Kähler: Schriften zu Christologie und Mission* (TB 42), Munich 1971, 21. See Dunn, *Jesus*, 560: "Here the point is that the core memory is of Jesus depicting his role in servant terms and commending it as an example to his core circle"; see also Wischmeyer, "Herrschen," 28.

29 M. Luther, *Von der Freiheit eines Christenmenschen*, in WA 7, (12), 21 (translation by Brian McNeil).

30 S. Vollenweider, *Freiheit als neue Schöpfung: Eine Untersuchung zur Eleutheria bei Paulus und in seiner Umwelt* (FRLANT 147), Göttingen 1989, 403.

31 Paul likewise says that he, as a free man, has made himself the slave of all, in order to win them (1 Cor 9:19).

32 Roloff, *Kirche*, 133. J. Roloff refers to texts such as 1 Thess 1:6; 1 Cor 11:1; and Phil 3:17.

33 See R. Feldmeier, *The First Letter of Peter: A Commentary on the Greek Text*, trans. Peter H. Davids, Waco, Tex., 2008, 217.

34 According to the testimony of the Acts of the Apostles, Peter too calls his apostleship a service (Acts 1:25; cf. 1:17).

35 Rom 1:1; Phil 1:1; cf. also Gal 1:10; 2 Cor 6:4.

36 Eph 6:5; 2 Tim 2:24.

37 2 Pet 1:1; Jas 1:1.

38 The serving can also refer to individual actions that are associated with a ministry in the community. For example, the collection of funds and the delivery of the collection to the community in Jerusalem is called a "service" of them (cf. Rom 15:31; 2 Cor 8:19-20; Acts 11:29; 12:25).

39 With regard to the gifts of the Spirit, E. Peterson is surely correct to observe, referring to 1 Cor 12:5, "it is not by chance that the concept of *diakonia* . . . is linked to the concept of the Kyrios. Behind this, there probably lies some kind of memory of logia such as: 'I have not come to be served, but to serve.' . . . Serving is an essential aspect of the Kyrios" (Peterson, *Korinther*, 286).

40 The "Ansbacher Ratschlag": see K. D. Schmidt, *Die Bekenntnisse und grundsätzlichen Äußerungen zur Kirchenfrage*. Vol. 2: *Das Jahr 1934*, Göttingen 1935, 102–4.

41 The fifth thesis of the Ansbach Memorandum runs as follows: "Recognizing this, we, as believing Christians, thank God the Lord that he has bestowed on our people in its distress the Führer as a 'pious and faithful overlord' and that he wishes to establish in the National Socialist ordering of the state a 'good governance,' a governance with 'discipline and honor.' We are therefore conscious of our responsibility before God to give aid to the work of the Führer in our profession and our social class." Schmidt, *Bekenntnisse*, 103.

42 Schmidt, *Bekenntnisse*, 103.

43 The following circumstances from Paul's time have been proposed: the earlier tumults under Claudius, which were relevant because, at roughly the period when Romans was written, those who had been expelled at that time were allowed to return to Rome (Wilckens, *Römer, 12–16*, 36); or the disturbances related by Tacitus (*Annals* 13.50-51) and Suetonius (*Nero* 10.1), directed against the collectors of taxes and customs duties (P. Stuhlmacher, *Der Brief an die Römer* [NTD 6], 15th ed., Göttingen 1998, 179–80). There is no evidence to support the conjecture that is sometimes put forward, to the effect that some of the Roman Christians sympathized with the resistance movement of the Zealots and that the apostle's remarks are directed against them.

44 *Phobos* is owed not to the human institutions but only to God (1 Pet 2:17); on this, see Feldmeier, *Peter*, 158–65.

45 On the connection to the context of the Letter to the Romans, see Stuhlmacher, *Römer*, 178; Wilckens, *Römer 6–11*, 30f.

46 The idea of *taxis* (order, arrangement) is manifested in the use of the corresponding verbs: the authorities are *ordained* or *set in order* by God (v. 1: *tetagmenai*; v. 2: *diatagê[i]*), and this is why the Christians should sub*ordinate* themselves to them (v. 1: *hupotassesthô*).

47 Soldiers such as the centurion in Capharnaum or Cornelius are not told to give up their profession; see also the sermon of the Baptist to the various social classes at Luke 3:14. On the problems as a whole, see M. Luther, *Ob Kriegsleute auch in seligem Stand sein können*, in WA 19, 623–62.

48 Plato, *Gorgias*, 517b. This expression has a negative connotation in Plato, since the "servants of the state" in the past to whom this term is applied were not ideal: they provided for the state only "that which it desired." In other words, their *pragmatikê diakonia* was concerned only about the needs of the body, and they did not improve the souls of human beings (517c-d).

49 P. Althaus, *Der Brief an die Römer* (NTD 6), 4th ed., Göttingen 1938; 13th ed. 1978, 111 (emphasis original). This restriction is not found in the thirteenth edition (1978). But when Paul Althaus says there that the "yes" of the apostle "does not apply to the tyrannical degeneration of the state, but to the state *per se* and as such" (133) and that even the question of resistance to the state cannot "simply be struck down by means of the exhortation to obedience in Rom 13" (135), this too must be understood as a clear correction of the Ansbach Memorandum.

50 It is pointless to speculate whether Paul would have formulated Romans 13 differently if those who held power had been Christians, but this seems improbable. When pagans in high positions become Christians, like the officer Cornelius in Acts 10 or the jail keeper in Acts 16, it is not expected that they will give up their profession after their conversion. The Baptist's sermon to the various social classes in Luke 3:12-14 shows that only the abuse of power was rejected.

51 See K. Barth, *Die kirchliche Dogmatik*. Vol. 2: *Die Lehre von Gott*, Zurich 1948 (*KD* 2/2), 806: The important thing is "to make it possible for human beings to live together in society, even under the presupposition that their life, which is contrary to the grace of God, is a life devoid of grace. In that case, grace itself must take on the form of the order of things that is devoid of grace, and sustain it" (translation by Brian McNeil).

52 This change from absolutized virtue to terror can be seen above all in the various revolutions from the French Revolution onward

and then once again in the Communist revolutions. This is true even where a state or a political movement appeals to God in justification of its actions.

53 Jesus' service includes both his "mighty deeds" (*dunameis*), which he performs with the authority that has been given to him, and his suffering. The Father's response to this will be his exaltation, as Jesus underlines in his final teaching dialogue in the temple (Mark 12:35-37) and once again at the lowest point of his life, when he is on trial before the high council (Mark 14:62). Here, the only name he now has for God is *Dunamis* (Power)—a power that does not bring low, but raises up. This is why he will return, exalted to the right hand of this Power. It is thus one and the same power of God that is at work both in Jesus' authoritative activity and in his dying and rising.

54 On this distinction between the ultimate and the penultimate, see D. Bonhoeffer, *Ethik* (DBW 6), Munich 1992, 137.

Chapter 3

1 *BJ* 4.9.2: The soldiers turn against the newly appointed Emperor Galba because of his avarice and his "shabbiness" (*tapeinophrosunê*), and slay him.

2 *Diss.* 3.24.56: "One who does not make himself dependent on things over which he has no power is not of a servile disposition (*tapeinophrosunê*)."

3 See the monograph by S. Rehrl, *Das Problem der Demut in der profangriechischen Literatur im Vergleich zu Septuaginta und Neuem Testament* (AeC 4), Münster 1961, esp. 196ff.; A. Dihle, art. "Demut," *RAC* 3 (1957): 735–78; A. Dihle, "Antike Höflichkeit und christliche Demut," *SIFC* 26 (1952): 169–90; on the history, see E. Zemmrich, *Demut: Zum Verständnis eines theologischen Schlüsselbegriffs* (EThD 4), Berlin 2006.

4 Col 3:12; Eph 4:2; Acts 20:19; 1 Pet 3:8; 5:5-6; cf. also Jas 1:10; 4:10.

5 See Grundmann, "*tapeinos*," esp. 6–15; Dihle, "Demut," 743–48.

6 Luke 14:11; 18:14 par. Matt 23:12; Matt 18:4.

7 See above.

8 Translation slightly altered in light of Sauer's translation.

9 Schlatter, "Demut," 35.

10 It is striking that Paul justifies this by a reference not to the earthly Jesus but to the self-abasement of the preexistent Jesus.

11 On the picture of Jesus in Matthew, which we encounter above all in Jesus' description of himself as "gentle and humble of

heart" in the tender invitation of the Savior (Matt 11:29), see chapter 2, above.

12 21.8; 30.8; 31.4; 44.3; 48.6; 56.1; 58.2.

13 Dihle, "Demut," 756.

14 P. Bahr, *Haltung zeigen: Ein Knigge nicht nur für Christen*, Gütersloh 2010, 100.

15 Something similar happens with regard to service where the concept of a "service community" is employed one-sidedly in the context of pay bargaining.

16 S. Kierkegaard, *Die Krankheit zum Tode: Der Hohepriester—der Zöllner—Die Sünderin*, 4th ed., Gütersloh 1992, 148 (translation by Brian McNiel).

17 F. Nietzsche, *Menschliches, Allzumenschliches I* (Sämtliche Werke 2), Munich 1980, Aph. 87: "an improvement on Luke 18:14."

18 F. Nietzsche, *Der Fall Wagner: Götzen-Dämmerung. Der Antichrist: Ecce homo. Dionysos-Dithyramben. Nietzsche contra Wagner* (Sämtliche Werke 6), Munich 1999, 43.

19 As early as the Letter to the Colossians, it is necessary to take a stand against people whom the author accuses of having a fleshly attitude, since they "puff themselves up" over against their fellow Christians by means of an asceticism that is called *tapeinophrosunê* (Col 2:18) and perhaps through the claim to possess a higher wisdom (Col 2:23). On the interpretation of these passages, which are not altogether easy to understand, see P. Pokorný, *Der Brief des Paulus an die Kolosser* (ThHNT 10/1), 2nd ed., Leipzig 1990, 123, 131–32.

20 The Letter to the Colossians distances itself from falsely understood humility; but the author finds it perfectly natural, only a few verses later (Col 3:12), to include humility among the foundations of Christian conduct (see below).

21 See G. Guttenberger Ortwein, *Status und Statusverzicht im Neuen Testament und seiner Umwelt* (NTOA 39), Freiburg 1999, 317. Despite occasional modifications to this picture, S. Rehrl too concludes, "The negative understanding of the word predominates everywhere in profane Greek literature" (*Demut*, 199).

22 *Diss.* 3.24.56; see also the diatribe on freedom, 4.1.54.

23 The most celebrated example is the passage in Plato's *Laws* (716a) that is subsequently adduced by Celsus in his argument against the Christian idea of humility (Origen, *C. Cels.*, 6.15). It is in this sense that Plutarch describes Epaminondas of Thebes running around "unanointed and lowly" on the day after he had

won a battle, in order to punish himself for his presumption (Plutarch, *Regum et imperatorum apophthegmata*, 193a).

24 Dihle, "Demut," 738; see 742: "The words *tapeinos, humilis,* and their derivatives are never associated with a positive verdict on a modest, appropriate attitude on the part of a human being *qua* ethical personality."

25 On this, see M. Lang, *Die Kunst des christlichen Lebens: Rezeptionsästhetische Studien zum lukanischen Paulusbild* (ABG 29), Leipzig 2008, 319–21.

26 H. Wojtkowiak, *Christologie und Ethik im Philipperbrief: Studien zur Handlungsorientierung einer frühchristlichen Gemeinde in paganer Umwelt* (FRLANT 243), Göttingen 2012, 155.

27 "The concept of 'lowliness' (*tapeinophrosunê*) . . . is employed in profane Greek literature only in a pejorative sense, because the fundamental renunciation of self-affirmation is alien to the Hellenistic-Roman world." W. Schrage, *Ethik des Neuen Testaments* (GNT 4), 5th ed., Göttingen 1989, 192.

28 H. I. Marrou, *Geschichte der Erziehung im Klassischen Altertum*, ed. E. Harder, trans. C. Beumann, Freiburg and Munich 1957, 26–27.

29 "Aein aristeuein kai hupeirokhon emmenai allôn" (Homer, *Il.* 6.208 = 11.784; translation by Brian McNeil).

30 The Middle Platonist Celsus explicitly takes objection to the Christians' unjustified appeal to Plato (Origen, *C. Cels.*, 6.15; cf. 3.61).

31 This is particularly noticeable in the case of *douleuein*, which, unlike other words for "serving" such as *latreuein, leitourgein,* or *hupêretein,* has "somewhat ignoble, servile" associations (Brandt, *Dienst*, 26).

32 See E. Lohmeyer, *Kyrios Jesus: Eine Untersuchung zu Phil. 2,5-11* (SHAW.PH 4 (1927/28), 2nd ed., Darmstadt 1962, 4–10. Most interpreters have followed Lohmeyer; see inter alia the recent commentaries by U. B. Müller, *Der Brief des Paulus an die Philipper* (ThK 11/1), 2nd ed., Leipzig 2002, 92–95; and N. Walter in N. Walter, E. Reinmuth, and P. Lampe, *Die Briefe an die Philipper, Thessalonicher und an Philemon* (NTD 8/2), Göttingen 1998, 56–58. In our present context, it is of only secondary interest to determine the original extent of the hymn and which additions derive from Paul. Verse 8c, in particular, is usually regarded as a Pauline addition; for a contrary view, see O. Hofius, *Der Christushymnus Philipper 2,6-11: Untersuchungen zu Gestalt und Aussage eines urchristlichen Psalms* (WUNT 17), Tübingen 1976, 4–12.

33 G. D. Fee notes in a number of exegetes who discuss the origin of this text "a discernible . . . swing back to Pauline authorship." Fee, *Paul's Letter to the Philippians* (NICNT), Grand Rapids and Cambridge 1995, 192–93.

34 It is only in this Letter that he gives a community a deeper insight into how he feels (Phil 1:23), and it is only from this community that he accepts support (Phil 4:10-15).

35 Paul employs here the metaphor of a "struggle," which he also applies to his own life.

36 The word *paraklêsis* is often translated as "exhortation," but "encouragement" fits better in the fourfold list. This is also the more common meaning of this term in Paul; on this, see also P. T. O'Brien, *The Epistle to the Philippians* (NIGTC), Grand Rapids 1991, 170–71.

37 This "also" is expunged by a number of textual witnesses to interpret the demand in the sense of total selflessness.

38 German: *ein gefundenes Fressen*, "something that can be taken without any effort." On this translation, see W. Foerster, art. "*harpagmos*," *ThWNT* 1, 472–73.

39 If the "consolation of love" refers to God the Father, as E. Lohmeyer (*Der Brief an die Philipper* [KEK 9,1], 14th ed., Göttingen 1974, 82), holds, the apostle would be presenting the entire Trinity here, to make it clear that the mercy of which the fourth section in the verse speaks, in the hendiadys "compassion and sympathy," is based not on human goodwill, which keeps on breaking down, but on the activity of God in the community and on the imprint that the community receives from this activity.

40 He also has recourse to the motif of joy, which runs throughout the entire Letter.

41 Rom 12:26; 15:5; 2 Cor 13:11; cf. Phil 4:2.

42 The Gospels speak in an analogous manner of *metanoia*; cf. also Rom 12:1-2. On *phronein* in Paul in general, see also Backhaus, "Lebensraum," 28–30.

43 Lohmeyer translates this term as "the togetherness of souls" (*Philipper*, 80).

44 This expression points back to Phil 1:27, where the apostle has expressed the expectation that the Philippians will "stand firm in one spirit, striving side by side with one soul for the faith of the Gospel."

45 1 Cor 4:6, 18-19; 5:2; 8:1; 13:4; cf. 2 Cor 12:20.

46 Bahr, *Haltung zeigen*, 107.

47 Accordingly, as M. Bockmuehl rightly observes, humility is "precisely *not* feigned or groveling, nor a sanctimonious or pathetic lack of self-esteem, but rather a mark of moral strength and integrity." Bockmuehl, *The Epistle to the Philippians* (BNTC 11), London 1998, 110.

48 This is the title that G. D. Fee gives to his exposition of this section.

49 See Schrage, *Ethik*, 192.

50 Walter et al., *Philipper*, 53.

51 See E. Käsemann, "Kritische Analyse von Phil. 2,5-11," *ZThK* 47 (1950): 313–60.

52 The phrase "in the Lord" occurs a further eight times.

53 Käsemann speaks of the "sphere of Christ's lordship" ("Analyse," 356); similar language is used by Müller, *Philipper*, 90. This means that the concept of virtue is at least imprecise with regard to humility, since what is involved is not the self-determination of the subject within an established value system but the relationship to Christ or to God that is mirrored in one's relationship to one's fellow human being.

54 "The norm of the right *phronein* is determined by the *en Khristô[i] Iêsou*." J. Gnilka, *Der Philipperbrief* (HThK 10/3), 4th ed., Freiburg 1987, 108.

55 The contrasting picture to this is the sin that dwells in the human person and exercises a heteronomous rule over him (Rom 7:18-23).

56 See M. Konradt, "Neutestamentliche Wissenschaft und Theologische Ethik," in *ZEE* 55/4 (2011), 275; K. Backhaus takes a similar position: "The noun [of the Pauline relationship between Christology and ethics] is 'in the locative.' It is 'Christ'" ("Lebensraum," 13).

57 In this sense, Käsemann revised his earlier remarks and subsequently acknowledged explicitly Christ's function as a model. E. Käsemann, *An die Römer* (NT 8a), 4th ed., Tübingen 1980, 369.

58 Backhaus, "Lebensraum," 21; see also Schrage, *Ethik*, 162–63.

59 The introduction in v. 5 ("in Christ") and the name of Jesus in v. 10 make it completely clear that the hymn is in fact speaking of Jesus Christ and of his story. The pattern "abasement-exaltation" also recalls the logion of Jesus, quoted several times in the Gospels, that the one who abases himself will be exalted (Luke 14:11; 18:14; Matt 21:31). What Jesus promised there has already become reality here in his own case.

60 The only exception is the mention of the crucifixion.

61 The spectrum extends from the *per aspera ad astra* of the ancient traditions about Heracles, via the Jewish wisdom speculation (see Müller, *Philipper*, 112), to the gnostic myth of the fall and ascent of the primal human being. Echoes of the Old Testament Servant of the Lord or the myth of the fallen angel of light have been detected (VitAd 12ff.; see Gnilka, *Philipperbrief*, 138–44). The imperial cult has often been suggested. In a recent essay, P. B. Smit mentions coins that were struck a few years previously in Philippi and thus were presumably still in circulation when Paul's Letter was written. These depict the deification of Augustus by another figure, the *divus Iulius*. Smit interprets this figure as the "genius populi romani [*sic*]." Smit, "A Numismatic Note on Phil 2:9-11," *BN* NF 149 (2011): 110.

62 J. Becker in J. Becker, H. Conzelmann, and G. Friedrich, *Die Briefe an die Galater, Epheser, Philipper, Kolosser, Thessalonicher und Philemon* (NTD 8), 17th ed., Göttingen 1990, 151; similarly, O'Brien, *Philippians*, 193–98.

63 See Wojtkowiak, *Christologie und Ethik*, 83–94.

64 M. Hengel, "Christologie und neutestamentliche Chronologie. Zu einer Aporie in der Geschichte des Urchristentums," in M. Hengel, *Studien zur Christologie* (Kleine Schriften IV), ed. C.-J. Thornton (WUNT 201), Tübingen 2006, 42.

65 On the meaning of *morphê*, see Käsemann, "Analyse," 328–31.

66 Wojtkowiak, *Christologie und Ethik*, 96.

67 Konradt, *Ethik*, 277.

68 Even less is it a question of "compensatory justice"; this, however, is the position taken by Müller, *Philipper*, 113.

69 See Hofius, *Christushymnus*, 51; Müller, *Philipper*, 109–10.

70 As O. Hofius convincingly demonstrates, the background to Phil 2:9-11 is the eschatological homage to Yahweh that is attested both in the prophetic tradition and in the Psalms. *Christushymnus*, 41–55. The idea of a submission on the part of the powers, which plays a constitutive role in the demonological interpretation, is found nowhere. *Katakhthonios* is "in the common parlance of the Roman period a very common designation of the deceased in the underworld: it is the translation of the Latin *Manes*." C.-H. Hunzinger, "Zur Struktur der Christus-Hymnen in Phil 2 und 1. Petr 3," in E. Lohse, C. Burchard, and B. Schaller, eds. *Der Ruf Jesu und die Antwort der Gemeinde* (Festschrift J. Jeremias), Göttingen 1970, 152.

71 K. Wengst, "'. . . einander durch Demut für vorzüglicher halten . . .' Zum Begriff Demut bei Paulus und in der paulinischen Tradition," in W. Schrage, ed. *Studien zum Text und zur Ethik des Neuen Testaments* (BZNW 47), Berlin and New York 1986, 437.

72 Walter et al., *Philipper*, 59.

73 On this, see M. Hengel, "'Setze dich zu meiner Rechten!' Die Inthronisation Christi zur rechten Gottes und Psalm 110,1," in M. Philonenko, ed. *Le trône de Dieu* (WUNT 69), Tübingen 1993, 108–94 (repr. M. Hengel, *Studien zur Christologie* [Kleine Schriften 4], ed. C.-J. Thornton [WUNT 201], Tübingen 2006, 281–367).

74 This means that "the counter-image of the ruler who exalts himself . . . in Phil 2:6-11" is not only "the Christ who abases himself" (S. Vollenweider, "Der 'Raub' der Gottgleichheit. Ein religionsgeschichtlicher Vorschlag zu Phil 2,6(-11)," *NTS* 45 [1999]: 431), but also the God who hands over his name to Jesus and thus shares his power with him (cf. 1 Cor 8:6).

75 One typical example of the overlooking of God in exegesis is the observation by J. Gnilka that the change of subject in the hymn can be explained "only by the interplay of two distinct ideas that have their basis in the history of religion and tradition," because otherwise the hymn "could have spoken of the ascent or return of the heavenly being." Against this view, it must be underlined that the only reason the exaltation of Christ does not call monotheism into question is that the sovereignty of the Son of God is due not to "the ascent or return of the heavenly being," but exclusively to what God does to the crucified Jesus (*Philipperbrief*, 125). On this, see also G. Theissen, *Die Religion der ersten Christen: Eine Theorie des Urchristentums*, 4th ed., Gütersloh 2008, 81–83.

76 Käsemann, "Analyse," 353.

77 See Gnilka, *Philipperbrief*, 130; G. Barth, *Der Brief an die Philipper* (ZBK 9), Zurich 1979, 41; Müller, *Philipper*, 110. It is of secondary importance for our present purposes whether these words are related to the homage paid to the *Kyrios* by the cosmic spheres or—as is more likely—they indicate the purpose of this homage.

78 Bockmuehl, *Philippians*, 148.

79 On this, see also W. Thüsing, *Per Christum in Deum*, 2nd ed., Münster 1969, 46–60.

80 See Feldmeier and Spieckermann, *God*, 66–91.

81 There is, by the way, a remarkable parallel to this in the second great New Testament hymn, the prologue to John. There it

is the Word, which was in the beginning with God and which was God (John 1:1-2), that, according to the celebrated affirmation about the incarnation, became flesh (John 1:14). In the same verse, which can also be interpreted as abasement or expropriation, the name "Father" is employed for the first time for God, and this name will play a determinative role in the rest of the Gospel. In this hymn too, the coming of the Son has the same goal: "to all who received him, who believed in his name, he gave power to become children of God" (John 1:12).

82 Müller, *Philipper*, 114. The promised exaltation is not the reward for servility, since the humble person takes the path that answers to the path God has taken to him. Humility and exaltation are two sides of one and the same coin. They are two elements of what it means to belong to the sphere of power of the God whose sovereignty is demonstrated by his exaltation of the lowly (cf. Luke 1:47-55).

83 It is in this sense that *1 Clement*, at a slightly later date, praises humility as the path of existential fellowship with the "Lord" Jesus Christ: "For Christ belongs to the humble [*tapeinophronountôn*], not to those who exalt themselves over his flock. The scepter of God's majesty, the Lord Jesus Christ, did not come with the pomp of pride or of arrogance, although he could have done so. No, he came in humility [*tapeinophronôn*]" (*1 Clem.* 16.1-2; translation by Brian McNeil).

84 "Christ's lordship, then, points forward to the praise of God in his character of Father. It actually reveals him as father, in particular as the Father of Christ" (O'Brien, *Philippians*, 251).

85 Rom 12:15, 16a: "Rejoice with those who rejoice, weep with those who weep. Have the same thing in mind [*phronountes*] among yourselves."

86 Rom 12:17: "Do not repay anyone evil for evil, but take thought for what is noble [*kala*] in the sight of all."

87 See Feldmeier and Spieckermann, *God*, 93–124.

88 The word *henotês* occurs in the New Testament only in Ephesians: here at 4:3 and once again at 4:13.

89 As in the hymn in Philippians, here too the world of images of the myth of the descent "into the lower parts of the earth" and the ascent "above all the heavens" is adopted (Eph 4:8-10) to find words for what the Letter has earlier called the "mystery" of God's saving "will" (Eph 1:9) or "the mystery of Christ" (Eph 3:3-4). The Letter to the Ephesians thus underlines the universality of the salvific action in Christ, who "fills the universe," but at the

same time goes on to explain the "gifts" brought by Christ (Eph 4:8) as the ecclesial ministries that bring about the "building up of the body" (Eph 4:12).

90 On the scholarly discussion, see Feldmeier, *Peter*, 32–38.

91 This has recently been emphasized anew by J. Herzer, *Petrus oder Paulus? Studien über das Verhältnis des Ersten Petrusbriefes zur paulinischen Tradition* (WUNT 103), Tübingen 1998.

92 The *homophrones* of 1 Pet 3:8 corresponds to *to auto phronête* or *to hen phronountes* in Phil 2:2. *Sumpatheis* in 1 Pet 3:8 corresponds to *sumpsukhoi* in Phil 2:2, *philadelphia* in 1 Pet 3:8 to *philadelphia* in Rom 12:10 and to *tên autên agapên ekhontes* in Phil 2:2. Finally, *tapeinophrones* corresponds to *tapeinophrosunê* in Phil 2:2 and to *tois tapeinois* in Rom 12:16.

93 1 Pet 2:13-17 is addressed to all, who are to be subject to the authorities; 2:18-25 to the slaves, who are to obey their masters; and 3:1-6 to the women, who are to submit to their husbands.

94 Cf. also Prov 29:33 LXX.

95 "'Be submissive' might be viewed as the subscript of the whole code (2:13.18; 3:1.5; cf. 5:5)." D. Balch, *Let Wives Be Submissive: The Domestic Code in 1 Peter* (SBL.MS 26), Atlanta 1981, 98.

96 See Feldmeier, *Peter*, 152–57.

97 L. Goppelt, *Der erste Petrusbrief* (KEK 12,1), Göttingen 1978, 223 (German: *zuvorkommend*).

98 These exhortations dominate the entire section from 1 Pet 2:12 onward and conclude with the final demand not to repay evil with evil (1 Pet 3:9/Rom 12:17) but, instead, to answer a curse with a blessing (1 Pet 3:9/Rom 12:14). The latter exhortation is the reason for the following quotation from Ps 34:13-17, which promises God's loving care to those whose behavior is marked by mercy, humility, and the willingness to forgive (1 Pet 3:10-12).

99 Goppelt, *Petrusbrief*, 333.

100 On the problems connected with these terms, see Feldmeier, *Peter*, 237–38.

101 On the reference that this exhortation makes to Mark 10:42-45, see Feldmeier, *Peter*, 235–36.

102 Apart from Mark 10:42 par. it is found in the New Testament only at Acts 19:16.

103 N. Brox, *Der erste Petrusbrief* (EKK 21), 4th ed., Zurich 1993, 236.

104 Goppelt, *Petrusbrief*, 336.

105 "The point is not that Christians have a choice of whether they humble themselves; that happens to them simply because they are Christians. The point is rather that the Christians are to

acknowledge that such a status conforms to God's will and to accept it for that reason, since it is the path God wishes Christians to take." P. J. Achtemeier, *A Commentary on First Peter* (Hermeneia), Minneapolis 1996, 338. A similar position is taken by K. H. Schelkle, *Die Petrusbriefe. Der Judasbrief* (HThK 13), Freiburg 2002, 131.

106 The author speaks at 1 Pet 4:11 of the power that God grants. At 5:10, he says that God "restores, supports, strengthens, and establishes."

107 This is vividly described in Psalm 91, which however speaks not of the hand of God but of his shadow and his wings.

108 J. H. Elliott, *1 Peter* (AncB 37B), New York 2000, 851.

109 F. Schnider, *Der Jakobusbrief* (RNT), Regensburg 1987, 34; a similar position is taken by R. P. Martin, *James* (WBC 48), Waco, Tex., 1988, 25; L. T. Johnson, *The Letter of James* (AncB 37A), New York 1995, 185.

110 S. Laws, *A Commentary on the Epistle of James* (BNTC 16), London 1980, 63.

111 Schnider, *Jakobusbrief*, 36; see H. Frankemölle, *Der Brief des Jakobus* (ÖTK 17/1–2), Würzburg 1994, 245.

112 See James 4:2-3; James goes so far as to say that the human being becomes a murderer.

113 "James is using the symbolism found in Torah for the covenantal relationship between Yahweh as groom and Israel as bride. The covenant was like a marriage (Isa 54:4-8) in which Israel's frequent infidelities could be considered as adultery (see LXX Ps 72:27; Jer 3:6-10; 13:27; Is 57:3; Hos 3:1; 9:1; Ezek 16:38; 23:45)" (Johnson, *James*, 278). At the same time, the contrast between two modes of existence basically constitutes an anthropological reformulation of the "two ways" motif that prefigures the Augustinian antithesis between *frui Deo* and *frui mundo*.

114 It has not proved possible to identify these words as a passage in Scripture, and many interpreters therefore hold that it is a quotation from a lost text. L. T. Johnson suggests that the passage should be understood as an introduction to the citation from scripture in v. 6b (see *James*, 280). It is worth bearing in mind H. Frankemölle's suggestion that the understanding of Scripture in the earliest Christian theology must not be limited to literal citations. Rather, "scripture" (as, e.g., in 1 Cor 15:3-5 or Luke 9:22; 17:25; 24:7, 26; and many other passages) indicates the "basic attitude and point of view that become normative" (*Jakobus*, 603).

115 This is also indicated by the aorist tense, which expresses one single event in the past—in this case, the creation of the human being. The passage would then mean that God "lays claim for himself alone to that which he has created and has bestowed on the human being as a gift. He does not tolerate it when the human being gives space in himself for other 'spirits.'" W. Schrage in H. Balz and W. Schrage, *Die "katholischen" Briefe: Die Briefe des Jakobus, Petrus, Johannes und Judas*, 14th ed., Göttingen and Zurich 1993, 46. See further E. Rückstuhl, *Jakobusbrief. 1.–3. Johannesbrief* (NEB 17/19), Würzburg 1985, 26; Schnider, *Jakobusbrief*, 101; and many others. It is possible that this is linked to the psychological interpretation of an impulse to the good that is inherent in the human being. This idea is found in some Jewish circles (see Johnson, *James*, 280–81; Schnider, *Jakobusbrief*, 101). The other possibility would be to understand the "spirit" as the Holy Spirit, whom God has bestowed on the believers as a gift (at baptism).

116 It is possible that this statement, which is formulated in the present tense, could belong to the quotation from an unknown scripture, but it is more probable that James has created it to form the transition to v. 6b.

117 Arist. 263; 1 Pet 5:1; *1 Clem.* 30.2; Ign. *Eph.* 5.3.

118 "As in the previous statement, this exhortation reveals a powerful optimism" (Johnson, *James*, 284). It is worth asking to what extent the Letter of James alludes here to the temptation narrative.

119 "The reader who is double-minded seeks to be friendly with the world and with God" (Martin, *James*, 154).

120 Balz and Schrage, *Jakobus*, 46.

121 Literally, "people with a double soul."

122 The aorist imperative (rather than a present imperative) may indicate that this is not a lasting self-diminution. It is rather a question of the seriousness of the unique conversion to God (thus Frankemölle, *Jakobus*, 613).

123 Frankemölle, *Jakobus*, 613.

124 H. Windisch, *Die katholischen Briefe* (HNT 15), 3rd ed., Tübingen 1951, 27–28; see Schrage, *Jakobus*, 44: "in the style of a preacher of repentance."

125 See the criticism by Celsus (Origen, *C. Cels.* 6.15). Dihle, "Demut," 737–43, presents examples from the patristic period.

126 "The strict hierarchical ordering of both spiritual and secular life does not lead to ossification, as long as the ideal of humility

poses a question mark against the definitiveness of all categories and gradations. . . . Last but not least: through this teaching about humility, the church was able to be at home in the world of late antiquity without abandoning its own self" (Dihle, "Demut," 759).

127 *Recommendatio humilitatis* 72, 75 (translation by Brian McNeil).

Chapter 4

1 Bonhoeffer, *Widerstand*, 535.

2 Bockmuehl, *Philippians*, 111. This is why, in his defense of humility, Chesterton provocatively emphasizes that the humble are those who are "secure" thanks to God's promise and who therefore know that they are empowered: "The pagans insisted upon self-assertion because it was the essence of their creed that the gods, though strong and just, were mystic, capricious, and even indifferent. But the essence of Christianity was in a literal sense the New Testament—a covenant with God which opened to men a clear deliverance. They thought themselves secure; they claimed palaces of pearl and silver under the oath and seal of the Omnipotent; they believed themselves rich with an irrevocable benediction which set them above the stars; and immediately they discovered humility. It was only another example of the same immutable paradox. It is always the secure who are humble." G. K. Chesterton, *The Defendant*, London 1901, chap. 12, "A Defense of Humility."

3 "Die selige Mutter Teresa," *PUR spezial*, 4th ed., Kisslegg 2010, 15 (translation by Brian McNeil).

Bibliography

Biblical Texts

B. Aland et al., ed. *Novum Testamentum Graece: Editio critica maior*, Stuttgart 1997–.

E. Nestle and B. Aland, eds. *Novum Testamentum Graece*, 27th ed., Stuttgart 2005.

A. Rahlfs and R. Hanhart, eds. *Septuaginta: Id est Vetus Testamentum Graece iuxta LXX interpretes*, Stuttgart 2006.

Septuaginta: Vetus Testamentum Graecum Auctoritate Academiae Litterarum Gottingensis, Göttingen 1926–.

Apocrypha

Translation: G. Sauer, *Jesus Sirach (Ben Sirach)* (JSHRZ III/5), Gütersloh 1981.

Parabiblical Literature

Letter of Aristeas (Arist.).

Text: P. Wendland, ed. *Aristeae ad Philocratem epistula. Cum ceteris de origine versionis LXX interpretum testimoniis* (BSGRT), Leipzig 1900.

Translation: R. H. Charles, ed. *The Apocrypha and Pseudepigrapha of the Old Testament in English*, vol. 2, Oxford 1913, 83–122.

Vita Adae et Evae (VitAd).

Translation: R. H. Charles, ed. *The Apocrypha and Pseudepigrapha of the Old Testament in English*, vol. 2, Oxford 1913, 123–54.

Ancient Sources

Ambrosiaster, *Quaestiones Veteris* (*QT*).

A. Souter, *Pseudo-Augustini: Quaestiones Veteris et Novi Testamenti CXXVII* (CSEL 50), Vienna and Leipzig 1908.

Augustine, *Confessiones* (*Conf.*).

L. Verheijen, ed. *Confessiones: Sancti Augustini Confessionum, libri XIII* (CChr.SL 27), Turnhout 1996.

———, *De genesi ad litteram* (*De gen. litt.*).

J. Zycha, *Sancti Aurelii Augustini: De Genesi ad litteram libri XII. Eiusdem libri capitula. De Genesi ad litteram imperfectus liber. Locutionum in Heptateuchum libri VII* (CSEL 28,1), Vienna 1894.

———, *In evangelium Ioannis* (*In ev. Ioan.*).

W. Radbodus, ed. *Sancti Aurelii Augustini opera VIII: In Johannis Evangelium tractatus CXXIV* (CChr.SL 24), Turnhout 1954.

Cicero, *De natura deorum.*

O. Plassberg and W. Ax, eds. *M. Tulli Ciceronis scripta quae manserunt omnia* (BSGRT), Stuttgart 1980.

Cleanthes, *Fragment* (*Frg.*).

J. ab Arnim, ed. *Stoicorum veterum fragmenta.* Vol. 1: *Zeno et Zenonis discipuli*, Leipzig 1921.

1 Clement (*1 Clem.*).

J. A. Fischer, ed. *Die Apostolischen Väter* (SUC 1), 10th ed., Darmstadt 2004 [= 1993].

Epictetus, *Dissertationes* (*Diss.*).

S. Schenkl, *Epicteti dissertationes* (BSGRT), Stuttgart 1965.

Flavius Josephus, *De bello Judaico* (*BJ*).

O. Michl and O. Bauernfeind, eds. *Flavius Josephus: De bello Judaico—Der jüdische Krieg.* 3 vols. Darmstadt 1959–1969.

Hesiod, *Works and Days.*

F. Solmsen, R. Merkelbach, and M. L. West, eds. *Hesiodi theogonia: Opera et dies. Scutum. Fragmenta selecta* (OCT), 3rd ed., Oxford 1990.

Greek text with translation: Hugh G. Evelyn-White, *Hesiod/Homeric Hymns/Epic Cycle–Homerica* (LCL 57), London 1914.

Homer, *Iliad* (*Il.*).

H. Rupé, ed. *Homer, Ilias: Griechisch und Deutsch*, 13th ed., Düsseldorf 2008.

Ignatius of Antioch, *Letters.*

J. A. Fischer, ed. *Die Apostolischen Väter* (SUC 1), 10th ed., Darmstadt 2004 [= 1993].

Marcus Minucius Felix, *Octavius* (*Oct.*).

B. Kytzler, ed. *M. Minucius Felix. Octavius. Lateinisch-Deutsch*, Munich 1965.

Menander of Athens, *Fragments* (*Frg.*).

Unus Multorum, *The Lately Discovered Fragments of Menander*, Oxford 1909.

Origen, *Contra Celsum* (*C. Cels.*).
J. M. Robinson, *The Philocalia of Origen*, Cambridge 1893.

Plato, *Laws*.
J. Burnet, *Platonis opera*. Vol. 5, Oxford 2006.

———, *Gorgias*.
J. Burnet, *Platonis opera*. Vol. 3, Oxford 2006.

Plutarch, *Regum et imperatorum apophthegmata*.
T. E. Page et al., ed. *Plutarch's Moralia. With an English Translation by P. H. de Lacy and B. Einarson et al.*, Cambridge 1959.

Polybius of Megalopolis, *Historiae*.
T. Büttner-Wobst, *Polybii historiae*. Vols. 1–4, Leipzig 1893–1905 (repr. Stuttgart 1962–1967).

Pseudo-Tertullian, *Carmen adversus Marcionitas* (*Car. adv. Marc.*).
K. Pollmann, ed. *Das carmen adversus Marcionitas: Einleitung, Text, Übersetzung und Kommentar* (Hyp. 96), Göttingen 1991.

Suetonius, *Nero*
Latin text with translation: J. C.Rolfe, *The Lives of the Caesars*. Vol. 2 (LCL), London, 1970.

Tacitus, *Annals*
Latin with translation: C. H. Moore and R. Jackson, *The Histories and the Annals*. Vol. 5 (LCL), London, 1968–1979.

Medieval Texts

Bernard of Clairvaux, *De consideratione ad Eugenium papam*.
J. Leclercq and H. M. Rochais, eds. *S. Bernardi opera*. Vol. 3: *Tractatus et opuscula* (editiones cistercienses), Rome 1963.

Thomas à Kempis, *Recommendatio humilitatis*.
F. Eichler, ed. *Thomas von Kempen, Lob der Demut*, in *De*

imitatione Christi und vier andere Schriften. Lateinisch-Deutsch, Munich 1966, 496–507.

Reformation

J. Kelly, *Paul Gerhardt's Spiritual Songs*, London 1867.

M. Luther, *Von der Freiheit eines Christenmenschen*, in WA 7, (12)20–38.

———, *Ob Kriegsleute auch in seligem Stand sein können*, in WA 19, 623–62.

Monographs

P. J. Achtemeier, *A Commentary on First Peter* (Hermeneia), Minneapolis 1996.

G. Alföldy, *Römische Sozialgeschichte*, 4th ed., Wiesbaden 2011.

P. Althaus, *Der Brief an die Römer* (NTD 6), 4th ed., Göttingen 1938; 13th ed. 1978.

R. Ambrosino, J. Heffernan, G. Shuttelsworth, and R. Ambrosino, *Social Work and Social Welfare: An Introduction*. Brooks/Cole Empowerment Series, 7th ed., Belmont, Calif., 2012.

M. Bachmann, *Göttliche Allmacht und theologische Vorsicht: Zu Rezeption, Funktion und Konnotationen des biblisch-frühchristlichen Gottesepithetons pantokrator* (SBS 188), Stuttgart 2002.

P. Bahr, *Haltung zeigen: Ein Knigge nicht nur für Christen*, Gütersloh 2010.

D. Balch, *Let Wives Be Submissive: The Domestic Code in 1 Peter* (SBL.MS 26), Atlanta 1981.

H. Balz and W. Schrage, *Die "katholischen" Briefe: Die Briefe des Jakobus, Petrus, Johannes und Judas*, 14th ed., Göttingen and Zurich 1993.

M. Barnes, *Taking Over the Asylum: Empowerment and Mental Health,* Toronto 1998.

G. Barth, *Der Brief an die Philipper* (ZBK 9), Zurich 1979.

K. Barth, *Die kirchliche Dogmatik.* Vol. 2: *Die Lehre von Gott.* 1st half volume, Zurich 1940 (*KD* 2/1).

———, *Die kirchliche Dogmatik.* Vol. 2: *Die Lehre von Gott.* 2nd half volume, Zurich 1948 (*KD* 2/2).

J. Becker, H. Conzelmann, and G. Friedrich, *Die Briefe an die Galater, Epheser, Philipper, Kolosser, Thessalonicher und Philemon* (NTD 8), 17th ed., Göttingen 1990.

K. Blanchard, J. P. Carlos, and A. Randolph, *The 3 Keys to Empowerment: Release the Power Within People for Astonishing Results,* San Francisco 2001.

M. Bockmuehl, *The Epistle to the Philippians* (BNTC 11), London 1998.

D. Bonhoeffer, *Ethik* (DBW 6), Munich 1992.

———, *Widerstand und Ergebung: Briefe und Aufzeichnungen aus der Haft* (DBW 8), Munich 1998.

W. Brandt, *Dienst und Dienen im Neuen Testament* (NTF [Reihe 2], Untersuchungen zum Kirchenproblem des Urchristentums 3), Gütersloh 1931.

N. Brox, *Der erste Petrusbrief* (EKK 21), 4th ed., Zurich 1993.

G. K. Chesterton, *The Defendant,* London 1901.

S. R. Covey, *The 7 Habits of Highly Effective People: Powerful Lessons in Personal Change,* New York 2004.

J. D. G. Dunn, *Jesus Remembered: Christianity in the Making.* Vol. 1, Grand Rapids and Cambridge 2003.

J. H. Elliott, *1 Peter* (AncB 37B), New York 2000.

G. D. Fee, *Paul's Letter to the Philippians* (NICNT), Grand Rapids and Cambridge 1995.

R. Feldmeier, *The First Letter of Peter: A Commentary on the Greek Text,* trans. Peter H. Davids, Waco, Tex., 2008.

R. Feldmeier and H. Spieckermann, *God of the Living: A Biblical Theology*, trans. Mark A. Biddle, Waco, Tex., 2011.

H. Frankemölle, *Der Brief des Jakobus* (ÖTK 17/1–2), Würzburg 1994.

J. Gnilka, *Das Evangelium nach Markus*. Vol. 2: *Mark 8,27–16,20* (EKK 2/2), Neukirchen-Vluyn 1979.

———, *Der Philipperbrief* (HThK 10/3), 4th ed., Freiburg 1987.

L. Goppelt, *Der erste Petrusbrief* (KEK 12,1), Göttingen 1978.

G. Guttenberger Ortwein, *Status und Statusverzicht im Neuen Testament und seiner Umwelt* (NTOA 39), Freiburg 1999.

U. Heckel, *Kraft in Schwachheit: Untersuchungen zu 2. Kor 10-13* (WUNT 2/56), Tübingen 1995.

A. Hentschel, *Diakonia im Neuen Testament: Studien zur Semantik unter besonderer Berücksichtigung der Rolle von Frauen* (WUNT 2/226), Tübingen 2007.

J. Herzer, *Petrus oder Paulus? Studien über das Verhältnis des Ersten Petrusbriefes zur paulinischen Tradition* (WUNT 103), Tübingen 1998.

O. Hofius, *Der Christushymnus Philipper 2,6-11: Untersuchungen zu Gestalt und Aussage eines urchristlichen Psalms* (WUNT 17), Tübingen 1976.

L. T. Johnson, *The Letter of James* (AncB 37A), New York 1995.

E. Käsemann, *An die Römer* (NT 8a), 4th ed., Tübingen 1980.

S. Kierkegaard, *Die Krankheit zum Tode: Der Hohepriester—der Zöllner—Die Sünderin*, 4th ed., Gütersloh 1992.

M. Lang, *Die Kunst des christlichen Lebens: Rezeptionsästhetische Studien zum lukanischen Paulusbild* (ABG 29), Leipzig 2008.

S. Laws, *A Commentary on the Epistle of James* (BNTC 16), London 1980.

H. G. Liddell and R. Scott, *A Greek-English Lexicon*, ed. H. S. Jones, 9th ed., Oxford 1983.

E. Lohmeyer, *Der Brief an die Philipper* (KEK 9,1), 14th ed., Göttingen 1974.

———, *Kyrios Jesus: Eine Untersuchung zu Phil. 2,5-11* (SHAW.PH 4 [1927/28]), 2nd ed., Darmstadt 1962.

H. I. Marrou, *Geschichte der Erziehung im Klassischen Altertum*, ed. E. Harder, trans. C. Beumann, Freiburg and Munich 1957.

R. P. Martin, *James* (WBC 48), Waco, Tex., 1988.

U. B. Müller, *Der Brief des Paulus an die Philipper* (ThK 11/1), 2nd ed., Leipzig 2002.

F. Nietzsche, *Der Fall Wagner: Götzen-Dämmerung. Der Antichrist. Ecce homo. Dionysos-Dithyramben. Nietzsche contra Wagner* (Sämtliche Werke 6), Munich 1999.

———, *Menschliches, Allzumenschliches I und II* (Sämtliche Werke 2), Munich 1980.

M. P. Nilsson, *Geschichte der griechischen Religion*. Vol. 1: *Die Religion Griechenlands bis auf die griechische Weltherrschaft* (HAW V,2,1), 3rd ed., Munich 1976.

P. T. O'Brien, *The Epistle to the Philippians* (NIGTC), Grand Rapids 1991.

R. Pesch, *Das Markusevangelium: Einleitung und Kommentar zu Kapitel 1,1-8,26* (HThK 2/1), Freiburg 1976.

———, *Das Markusevangelium: Einleitung und Kommentar zu Kapitel 8,24-16,20* (HThK 2/2), Freiburg 1977.

E. Peterson, *Der erste Brief an die Korinther und Paulus-Studien: Aus dem Nachlass herausgegeben von Hans-Ulrich Weidemann* (Ausgewählte Schriften 7), Würzburg 2006.

P. Pokorný, *Der Brief des Paulus an die Kolosser* (ThHNT 10/1), 2nd ed., Leipzig 1990.

S. R. F. Price, *Rituals and Power: The Roman Imperial Cult in Asia Minor*, Cambridge 2002 (1984).

S. Rehrl, *Das Problem der Demut in der profangriechischen*

Literatur im Vergleich zu Septuaginta und Neuem Testament (AeC 4), Münster 1961.

J. Roloff, *Die Kirche im Neuen Testament* (NTD Ergänzungsreihe 10), Göttingen 1993.

E. Rückstuhl, *Jakobusbrief. 1.-3. Johannesbrief* (NEB 17/19), Würzburg 1985.

J. Rüpke, *Die Religion der Römer: Eine Einführung*, 3rd ed., Munich 2006.

M. Scheler, *Der Genius des Krieges und der deutsche Krieg*, 3rd ed., Leipzig 1917.

K. H. Schelkle, *Die Petrusbriefe. Der Judasbrief* (HThK 13), Freiburg 2002.

K. D. Schmidt, *Die Bekenntnisse und grundsätzlichen Äußerungen zur Kirchenfrage.* Vol. 2: *Das Jahr 1934*, Göttingen 1935.

R. Schnackenburg, *Die sittliche Botschaft des Neuen Testaments.* Vol. 1: *Von Jesus zur Urkirche* (HThK.S 1), Freiburg i.B. 1986.

U. Schnelle, *Einleitung in das Neue Testament*, 5th ed., Göttingen 2005.

F. Schnider, *Der Jakobusbrief* (RNT), Regensburg 1987.

W. Schrage, *Ethik des Neuen Testaments* (GNT 4), 5th ed., Göttingen 1989.

T. Söding, *Das Liebesgebot bei Paulus: Die Mahnung zur Agape im Rahmen der paulinischen Ethik* (NTA 26), Münster 1995.

H. L. Strack and P. Billerbeck, *Kommentar zum Neuen Testament aus Talmud und Midrasch.* Vol. 1: *Das Evangelium nach Matthäus*, 2nd ed., Munich 1956.

P. Stuhlmacher, *Der Brief an die Römer* (NTD 6), 15th ed., Göttingen 1998.

G. Theissen, *Die Religion der ersten Christen: Eine Theorie des Urchristentums*, 4th ed., Gütersloh 2008.

H. Thielicke, *Zwischen Gott und Satan: Die Versuchung Jesu und die Versuchlichkeit des Menschen*, Wuppertal 1968.

W. Thüsing, *Per Christum in Deum*, 2nd ed., Münster 1969.

J. P. Vernant, *Myth and Thought among the Greeks*, London 1983.

S. Vollenweider, *Freiheit als neue Schöpfung: Eine Untersuchung zur Eleutheria bei Paulus und in seiner Umwelt* (FRLANT 147), Göttingen 1989.

N. Walter, E. Reinmuth, and P. Lampe, *Die Briefe an die Philipper, Thessalonicher und an Philemon* (NTD 8/2), Göttingen 1998.

U. von Wilamowitz-Moellendorff, *Der Glaube der Hellenen*. Vol. 1, Darmstadt 1976.

U. Wilckens, *Der Brief an die Römer*. Vol. 2: *Römer 6–11* (EKK 6/2), Neukirchen-Vluyn 1980.

———, *Der Brief an die Römer*. Vol. 3: *Römer 12–16* (EKK 6/3), Neukirchen-Vluyn 1982.

H. Windisch, *Die katholischen Briefe* (HNT 15), 3rd ed., Tübingen 1951.

A. Wlosok, *Rom und die Christen: Lateinische Quellentexte zur Auseinandersetzung zwischen Christentum und römischem Staat*, Stuttgart 2002.

H. Wojtkowiak, *Christologie und Ethik im Philipperbrief: Studien zur Handlungsorientierung einer frühchristlichen Gemeinde in paganer Umwelt* (FRLANT 243), Göttingen 2012.

E. Zemmrich, *Demut: Zum Verständnis eines theologischen Schlüsselbegriffs* (EThD 4), Berlin 2006.

Articles in Periodicals and Lexica

K. Backhaus, "Evangelium als Lebensraum: Christologie und Ethik bei Paulus," in U. Schnelle, T. Söding, and

M. Labahn, eds. *Paulinische Christologie: Exegetische Beiträge* (Festschrift H. Hübner), Göttingen 2000, 9–31.

F. Bilabel, "Fragmente aus der Heidelberger Papyrussammlung," *Philologus* 80 (1925): 331–41.

A. Dihle, "Antike Höflichkeit und christliche Demut," *SIFC* 26 (1952): 169–90.

———, art. "Demut," *RAC* 3 (1957): 735–78.

E. Ebel, "Die Reisebegleiter und Mitarbeiter des Paulus," in O. Wischmeyer, ed. *Paulus: Leben—Umwelt—Werk—Briefe*, 2nd ed., Tübingen 2012, 124–28.

R. Feldmeier, "Das Lamm und die Raubtiere. Tiermetaphorik und Machtkonzeptionen im Neuen Testament," in R. Gebauer and M. Meiser, eds. *Die bleibende Gegenwart des Evangeliums* (Festschrift O. Merk, MThSt 76), Marburg 2003, 205–11.

W. Foerster, art. "*exestin ktl.*," *ThWNT* 2 (1935): 557–72.

———, art. "*harpagmos*," *ThWNT* 1 (1957): 472–74.

W. Grundmann, art. "*tapeinos ktl.*," *ThWNT* 8 (1969): 1–27.

B. Heininger, "'Politische Theologie' im Markusevangelium: Der Aufstieg Vespasians zum Kaiser und der Abstieg Jesu am Kreuz," in C. Mayer, ed. *Augustinus Ethik und Politik: Zwei Würzburger Augustinus-Studientage. Aspekte der Ethik bei Augustinus (11. Juni 2005). Augustinus und die Politik (24. Juni 2006)* (Cassiciacum 39,4 = Res et signa. Augustinus-Studien 4), Würzburg 2009, 171–201.

M. Hengel, "Christologie und neutestamentliche Chronologie: Zu einer Aporie in der Geschichte des Urchristentums," in M. Hengel, *Studien zur Christologie* (Kleine Schriften IV), ed. C.-J. Thornton (WUNT 201), Tübingen 2006, 27–51.

———, "'Setze dich zu meiner Rechten!' Die Inthronisation Christi zur rechten Gottes und Psalm 110,1," in M. Philonenko, ed. *Le trône de Dieu* (WUNT 69), Tübingen 1993,

108–94 (repr. M. Hengel, *Studien zur Christologie* [Kleine Schriften 4], ed. C.-J. Thornton [WUNT 201], Tübingen 2006, 281–367).

H. Hommel, "Der bald erhöhn, bald stürzen kann," in H. Hommel, *Sebasmata: Studien zur antiken Religionsgeschichte und zum frühen Christentum*. Vol. 2 (WUNT 32), Tübingen 1984, 3–10.

C.-H. Hunzinger, "Zur Struktur der Christus-Hymnen in Phil 2 und 1. Petr 3," in E. Lohse, C. Burchard, and B. Schaller, eds. *Der Ruf Jesu und die Antwort der Gemeinde* (Festschrift J. Jeremias), Göttingen 1970, 142–56.

M. Kähler, "Der Menschensohn und seine Sendung an die Menschheit," in H. Frohnes, ed. *Martin Kähler: Schriften zu Christologie und Mission* (TB 42), Munich 1971, 3–43.

E. Käsemann, "Kritische Analyse von Phil. 2,5-11," *ZThK* 47 (1950): 313–60.

M. Konradt, "Gott oder Mammon. Besitzethos und Diakonie im frühen Christentum," in C. Sigrist, *Diakonie und Ökonomie: Orientierung im Europa des Wandels* (Beiträge zu Theologie, Ethik und Kirche 1), Zurich 2006, 107–54.

———, "Neutestamentliche Wissenschaft und Theologische *Ethik*," in *ZEE* 55/4 (2011), 274–86.

———, "'Whoever humbles himself like this child. . .': The Ethical Instruction in Matthew's Community Discourse (Matt 18) and Its Narrative Setting," in R. Zimmermann and J. G. v.d. Watt, eds. *Moral Language in the New Testament: The Interrelatedness of Language and Ethics in Early Christian Writings*. Vol. 2 (WUNT [Reihe 2] 296), Tübingen 2010, 105–38.

S. R. F. Price, "Gods and Emperors: The Greek Language of the Roman Imperial Cults," *Journal of Hellenic Studies* 104 (1984): 79–95.

A. Schlatter, "Jesu Demut, ihre Missdeutungen, ihr Grund," *BFChTh* 8, Gütersloh 1904, 35–93.

"Die selige Mutter Teresa," *PUR spezial*, 4th ed., Kisslegg 2010.

P. B. Smit, "A Numismatic Note on Phil 2:9-11," *BN* NF 149 (2011): 101–12.

S. Vollenweider, "Der 'Raub' der Gottgleichheit: Ein religionsgeschichtlicher Vorschlag zu Phil 2,6(-11)," *NTS* 45 (1999): 413–33.

K. Wengst, "'. . . einander durch Demut für vorzüglicher halten . . .' Zum Begriff Demut bei Paulus und in der paulinischen Tradition," in W. Schrage, ed. *Studien zum Text und zur Ethik des Neuen Testaments* (BZNW 47), Berlin and New York 1986.

O. Wischmeyer, "Herrschen als Dienen—Markus 10,41-45," *ZNW* 90 (1999): 28–44.

E. Zenger, "I. Überlieferung und Entstehung des Buches," in E. Zenger, *Das Buch Judit* (JSHRZ 1/6), Gütersloh 1981, 429–31.

Index